The North American Securities Administrators Association
and
The Council of Better Business Bureaus

INVESTOR ALERT!

How To Protect Your Money From Schemes, Scams, and Frauds

A BENJAMIN BOOK

Andrews and McMeel
A Universal Press Syndicate Company
Kansas City • New York

1988

TO GET ADDITIONAL COPIES

Single copies of this book are available from your local bookstore, local Better Business Bureau (see Appendix A for addresses), or the Council of Better Business Bureaus, 1515 Wilson Boulevard, Arlington, VA 22209.

Special Discounts for Quantity Purchases

Special discounts for bulk quantities are offered to business firms, associations, government agencies, and other organizations that plan to use this title as a promotional, educational, or public relations tool. On orders of 1,000 or more copies, back cover identification and message are available, subject to approval of CBBB and NASAA. Contact: The Benjamin Company, One Westchester Plaza, Elmsford, NY 10523 Telephone: (914) 592-8088.

Author: Wilbur Cross
Editor: Virginia Schomp
Project Manager-CBBB: Stephen Jones
Project Manager-NASAA: Martin Weber
Editorial Assistant: Maura May
Designer: Pam Forde Graphics
Illustrator: Bill Colrus/Joseph, Mindlin & Mulvey
Typographer: David E. Seham Associates Inc.

Produced by The Benjamin Company, Inc.
    One Westchester Plaza
    Elmsford, NY 10523

Library of Congress Cataloging-in-Publication Data
Investor alert!
    "A Benjamin book."
    Includes index.
    1. Investments—Handbooks, manuals, etc
I. North American Securities Administrators
Association. II. Council of Better Business Bureaus.
HG4527.I583   1988   332.6'78   87-73235
ISBN 0-87502-228-6
ISBN 0-87502-230-8 (pbk.)
ISBN 0-87502-231-6 (mass market pbk.)
ISBN 0-8362-2226-1 (Andrews and McMeel)
ISBN 0-8362-2211-3 (Andrews and McMeel : pbk.)

Contents

	Preface		4
Chapter 1	**INVESTIGATE BEFORE YOU INVEST**		6
Chapter 2	**BUSINESS OPPORTUNITY—FOR WHOM?**		16
Chapter 3	**INVESTING IN COMMODITIES AND FUTURES**		28
Chapter 4	**PROBLEM-FREE FINANCIAL PLANNING**		40
Chapter 5	**FOOL'S GOLD AND OTHER "VALUABLES"**		54
Chapter 6	**LURE OF THE LAND**		68
Chapter 7	**PAINFUL DRILLING**		80
Chapter 8	**PENNY STOCKS—ARE THEY WORTH IT?**		92
Chapter 9	**PONZIS AND PYRAMIDS**		104
Chapter 10	**TIME-SHARING OR TIME-SHAVING?**		118
Chapter 11	**THE COME-ON IN BONDS**		130
Chapter 12	**BOILER ROOMS**		140
Chapter 13	**HOW TO SELECT AND DEAL WITH A STOCKBROKER**		156
	Conclusion		168
	Glossary of Terms		173
Appendix A	**Directory of BBB Offices**		178
Appendix B	**Directory of NASAA Offices**		184
Appendix C	**Directory of Government Agencies and Associations**		188
	Index		191

Preface

Americans lose hundreds of millions of dollars every year to investment fraud. It touches all segments of society: the rich and the poor, the young and the old. No one is immune. Swindlers and con artists prey on the hopes of us all. They will steal as readily from those in pursuit of the modest goal of financial security as from those who dream of great wealth.

The allies of the swindlers are ignorance and greed. Investment frauds are fueled by the swindlers' knowledge that people generally do not understand what is being offered to them and hear only the promise that they can make a great deal of money easily and quickly by handing over their savings to the promoters.

Once the money is in the hands of the swindlers, it is usually gone for good. Even if the promoters are arrested and convicted, there is often nothing left to give back to the victims. This means that it is vitally important for investors to protect themselves before money changes hands.

The Better Business Bureaus and the state securities administrators in the U.S. have seen this story repeated thousands of times. Lured by promises of high returns or huge tax savings, far too many investors plunge into fraudulent investments without investigating first. The same scams are worked over and over again on people who do not take the time to check out the offers or learn the danger signs.

The purpose of this book is to alert investors to the methods of operation, the typical pitches, and the danger signs of investment fraud. The sponsors of this book are the North American Securities Administrators Association, the organization of state officials who administer and enforce the securities laws at the grass roots level, and the Council of Better Business Bureaus, the international headquarters organization for Better Business Bureaus. This book is not an attempt to tell the public how to invest their money, but rather to give them the tools to discriminate between legitimate and fraudulent investments and to choose those investments that may be appropriate for them. In today's marketplace, this is not an easy task.

The deregulation of a large part of the financial market has let loose a proliferation of investment vehicles that are complicated and baffling, even to experts. Con artists have been equally prolific in coming up with new scams to fleece the public. Often it is very difficult to distinguish a legitimate investment opportunity from a scam. Nevertheless, investors are not defenseless. This book provides chapter-by-chapter descriptions and examples of how frauds work and ways of identifying potentially fraudulent deals. It is hoped that this advice will enable investors to avoid the costly lessons taught to thousands of Americans every year by fraudulent promoters who are ready, willing, and able to steal their money.

JAMES H. MCILHENNY
President, CBBB

JAMES C. MEYER
President, NASAA

5

Chapter 1
INVESTIGATE BEFORE YOU INVEST

The first widespread signal of financial disaster came in late April 1983, when major newspapers across the country reported that the International Gold Bullion Exchange in Fort Lauderdale, Florida, had been closed by court order because it presented an "imminent and substantial threat to the public welfare."

Characteristic of the announcement was the headline in the *New York Times* on April 25: BULLION DEALER'S CLOSING SPARKS INVESTOR WORRY. As the *Times* pointed out, "The shutdown came after hundreds of complaints and scores of lawsuits about undelivered gold, silver, and platinum prompted the Florida Attorney General's office to ask a Broward County Circuit Court judge to close the exchange." The order to stop doing business affected an estimated 1,000 employees, not only in Florida, but in Dallas and Los Angeles, where IGBE also maintained its offices.

The people who suddenly found themselves without jobs were but a handful of victims compared with the more than 25,000 reported customers who had unwisely and inadvertently poured money into a venture that would later be declared an outright fraud. For many of the stunned investors, the news was almost unbelievable. In a matter of only three years, the exchange had become one of the nation's largest retailers of precious metals, having started as a small storefront jewelry shop run by two ambitious brothers, William and James Alderdice. When William boasted to reporters and potential investors that he was going to create "the biggest business on the planet," his words were credible. For with annual sales of some $80 million, he had already demonstrated that he had the Midas touch.

Investors were lured with almost ridiculous ease by compelling television commercials and ads splashed across such prestigious newspapers as the *Wall Street Journal* and the *New York Times,* as well as countless other periodicals. Skeptics who questioned how it was possible that IGBE could offer gold and silver purchasers so much more for their money than other precious metals exchanges were shouted down by investors who were convinced that the exchange had conceived a magic formula. That formula was based on the idea that investors could purchase metals at discount prices as long as they were willing to go along with a "delayed delivery" program. The longer customers waited for delivery, the lower the prices they would pay for gold, silver, and platinum (Take your pick!).

The strategy allegedly was to sell gold and silver at one price and then purchase the same amounts at a much lower price in the future. "Rebate checks" were mailed monthly to customers as assurance that their investments were already earning money. Few of the recipients worried that the sums received were a mere 2.5 percent or less of their total investment. The Alderdices and their glib salespeople had a ready answer for most of the customers who did protest or who wanted to receive shipments of the precious metals that were supposedly being held for safekeeping in their accounts. They claimed, falsely, that high interest rates were being earned with investors' funds, thus enabling IGBE to invest its capital profitably and continue to offer its prized customers the kinds of astonishing discounts that no other bullion exchange could afford.

What it all amounted to was that customers were constantly peppered with advice to sit back and wait, defer delivery, and benefit from their patience. If they could hold out for 12 to 15 weeks, they would be well rewarded. The most insistent customers often did receive their gold and silver. However, many of those fell prey to dreams of riches and bought right back into the scheme.

For most investors, however, delivery never did come—and never would. A typical case was that of St. Michael's Church of

Life in Bristol, Connecticut, which raised $278,000 from its congregation for a new chapel and invested in IGBE in the hope of increasing the sum dramatically. The collapse of the exchange left the parish broke. "These days," said a report at the time, "the congregation meets in a rented hall on Sunday mornings and prays for a miracle."

Among the 25,000 customers who lost an estimated total of $300 million were many whose lives would be shattered by their unfortunate choice of investment. One such victim was a 52-year-old divorcée from Texas who was talked into investing her total savings, $46,000, in the hope that the unbelievable profits coming her way would enable her to move from a mobile home to a mini-mansion. When IGBE collapsed, she could no longer afford even the trailer.

The tragic part of this story of a boom that never happened and a bust that was preordained was that the warning signals were obvious to anyone not blinded by flashing dreams of easy riches. Almost a year before the Florida Attorney General began to crack down on the Alderdice brothers, *Forbes* magazine published an editorial that focused on one very basic question: "How can the International Gold Bullion Exchange retail gold and silver coins to the public so cheaply, often at spot market prices, pay for an expensive advertising campaign, and still earn a profit?"

Not only that, the article pointed out, but the company was pouring money into extravagantly appointed offices, leasing Learjets at $13,000 per flight so its executives could go on West Coast jaunts, and making it possible for its officers to purchase posh homes in Florida, California, and Texas. As one Wall Street gold trader, referring to the Alderdices' formula for success, said to the *Forbes* reporter, "If you find out how they do it, let me know."

For those who cared to investigate the nature of the investment that was tempting them, there were plenty of "Keep Out" signs. For one thing, the Alderdice brothers had a somewhat shady past, including arrest records for assault, vagrancy, indecent exposure, and writing bad checks. They were known to favor a jet-set style of life, with an abundance of expensive cars, fur-draped female companions, and expensive tastes in food and liquor. And would-be investors could hardly have been reassured by William's disturbing history of business failures and penchant for dabbling in questionable ventures in real estate, yacht brokering, and even a gold mine.

A few inquiries to the Better Business Bureau (BBB), North American Securities Administrators Association (NASAA), any of the 50 state Securities Divisions, or other agencies that are constantly on the alert for fraudulent get-rich-quick schemes would have saved thousands of IGBE investors millions of dollars. Unfortunately, victims seldom realize what has hit them until it is too late. One court-appointed investigator unearthed a significant piece of evidence that symbolized the Alderdice operations. Rooting around in the company vault, he came upon a pile of what looked like 40 bars of bullion. Closer inspection revealed that they were slabs of wood, painted bright gold.

No "Safe Bets"

Despite the adverse publicity following the downfall of the International Gold Bullion Exchange, a survey taken by NASAA and the Council of Better Business Bureaus (CBBB) revealed that other companies were offering by telephone and advertisement the same kind of deferred delivery of precious metals. That in itself does not mean that these firms are all dishonest. Yet a disturbing percentage of them use questionable methods and some have been subject to court actions and restrictions stemming from consumer complaints and the discovery of irregularities.

The lure of gold has literally shaped the history of our civilization, from the time when early tribes first discovered its beauty, its mystique, and its universal value. Is it any wonder, then, that con men and rip-off artists of many genres should use it as bait for their schemes? You will learn more about fool's gold, silver-plated frauds, and platinum-seeded swindles in chapter 5 of this book.

"If gold is something to invest in only with the utmost care," says the cautious investor, "then perhaps I would be wise to confine my objectives to real estate, looking for the best government bonds, or other more conservative and traditional investments." While this argument may appear to be sound, it is by no means a guarantee that you will thereby avoid the pitfalls, scams, and swindles that can endanger almost any kind of substantial investment.

Recently, some 300 investors in 20 states and several foreign countries contributed a total of almost $7 million to a plan that promised them shares of profits from 72 oil wells in southern Illinois. They learned too late that they had been bilked out of most of their investment, when a federal grand jury indicted the promoters of the scheme on more than 700 counts of mail and wire fraud and conspiracy to peddle unregistered securities. The wells existed all right, but contrary to exaggerated drilling claims, the productivity of most of them was negligible and the rights to the few that did have commercial production value were held by the Illinois couple engineering the swindle. While the 300 investors were pouring their money down the drain, the operators of the scheme were diverting the funds into expensive cars, a jet plane, a helicopter, and various luxuries to which they felt their ingenuity entitled them.

By comparison with investing in the volatile and sometimes risky commodities market, putting your money in a so-called "tax shelter" might seem like a pretty safe bet. Since the promoters of such schemes often assert that you can write off as much as $4 or $5 as a tax deduction for every $1 you invest, the temptation is great. How can you lose? As an additional incentive, you are assured that—though the venture is somewhat speculative—you stand to receive a windfall when the clever entrepreneur's business starts making profits.

One typical tax shelter swindle urged prospective investors to "get in on the ground floor of the burgeoning pop record business." The idea was that investors would own shares in the production of cassettes to be sold by the hundreds of thousands to manufacturers of stereo equipment, who would use them as premiums to help sell their products. As the promoter explained, even the profits that investors could expect would be deductible and could be averaged out over a period of years. What they did not bother to reveal was that the whole cassette scheme was fraudulent to begin with and that not a single manufacturer had been approached as a prospective buyer of cassettes for use as premiums. As several large investors later discovered to their chagrin, the IRS not only disallowed the illegal deductions but imposed stiff fines, penalties, and interest on back taxes.

The moral of these examples and others you will read about in the following pages is that everybody with money to spend should heed the long-standing advice of the CBBB: INVESTIGATE BEFORE YOU INVEST. Often a single phone call or a brief letter of inquiry will alert you to a financial disaster in the making, in time for you to avoid becoming involved. The CBBB, in conjunction with NASAA, helps investors anticipate frauds, scams, swindles, and other money-related problems by publicizing the following cautionary guidelines, which should be heeded no matter what form of investment you are considering.

Ten Do's and Don'ts For Investors

- Be wary of unexpected phone calls, letters, or even personal visits from strangers who offer quick-profit schemes that require your immediate investment.

- Look with doubt on promises that you can double your money or even expect a high return on your investment within a short period of time.

- Turn down money requests accompanied by high-pressure warnings like "Tomorrow will be too late" or "Act now because there will soon be a long waiting list of others who want to take advantage of this golden opportunity."

- Always demand *written* information about the organization behind the investment plan and its past track record. But bear in mind that even printed documents can easily be created, forged, or falsified.

- Be suspicious of "inside information," hot tips, and rumors that supposedly will give you a big advantage over other, less knowledgeable investors.

- Ask for a prospectus, offering circular, financial statement, or other similar document before you even consider investing. Then read the small print carefully and make sure you understand the terms thoroughly before signing any kind of commitment.

- Before making a commitment, get a professional opinion from your attorney, stockbroker, accountant, or other reliable consultant.

- Check with your Better Business Bureau, state securities administrator, or appropriate government agency to confirm that the company or individual is properly licensed to conduct the business in question and has no history of violating the law. Whenever possible, deal with established businesses whose reputations are known and respected in your community.

ALERT!

- When in doubt, make no promises or commitments, no matter how tentative. It is far better to wait and lose an opportunity than to take the plunge and lose everything.

- When hounded on the phone by a promoter, don't be afraid to hang up without explanation. You do not owe the caller anything—in fact this kind of solicitation is an invasion of your privacy.

Chapter 2

BUSINESS OPPORTUNITY —FOR WHOM?

ALERT!

The opportunity to invest in a franchise seemed to be exactly what Carol and Allen were looking for, a chance to break out of the endless commuting rat race and gradually establish a business that they could operate out of their own home. All they had to do was invest $4,000 for an initial supply of a brand-new window-washing compound that left glass crystal-clear and unstreaked. The investment guaranteed "an exclusive territory, sales literature, and participation in a forthcoming national ad campaign that would quickly make the product a 'best-seller.' "

At first skeptical when they received a "cold" telephone call, they were quickly convinced after the stranger at the other end of the line talked them into letting him pay a visit, during which he demonstrated the "space-age" product (which supposedly was used to clean portholes and instruments in spacecraft) and displayed advance proofs from the advertising program. As he explained it, Allen and Carol did not even have to store or process their supply of washing fluid. It would be kept, safe and sealed, in containers in the company warehouse. All they had to do was take orders from local supermarkets and hardware stores, maintain the books, and collect the payments. The deluge of orders, of course, would follow as soon as the ad campaign started to run and store buyers spotted their names as the sole distributors for the product in their area.

What the young couple particularly liked about the plan was that they could begin in a modest way, continue with their respective jobs, and then phase into their own business when they were ready to become full-time entrepreneurs. "If, for any reason, you find that you don't like the business," they were assured, "we can always find someone else to take over your territory and purchase the unsold remainder of your supplies. After all, the liquid retains its strength in storage forever, in sealed 50-gallon drums. There is no depreciation."

Not only was there no depreciation—there was no supply. The warehouse receipts handed to Allen and Carol in return for their $4,000 were falsified copies of receipts for a single shipment of drums delivered to a warehouse in the name of the operators of the scheme—just enough to establish the required documentation. Other would-be entrepreneurs taken in by the scheme had received copies suitably altered for their eyes alone.

The operators of this swindle were later arrested and indicted for fraud, evidenced by their having few supplies, no advertising contracts, and no evidence that they intended to develop even the most rudimentary window-cleaning business. By this time, however, the money taken in from distributors-to-be had largely vanished and few of those who had been bilked were able to recoup any of their original investment.

Both Sides of the Coin

Today, more than 10 million Americans and Canadians earn income from legitimate franchises and small-business opportunities. The United States Department of Commerce estimates that independent salespeople contribute almost $9 billion annually to the U. S. economy and that franchises alone account for about one-third of all retail sales.

Under the circumstances, the abundance of business opportunities forms a bright montage for would-be entrepreneurs who want the freedom to work on their own and to have more control over their lives than if they were employed by someone else. They can select their field of endeavor from an astonishing array of businesses, ranging from the conventional to the exotic, in places as remote as the wilderness forests of the Northwest to the urban crunch of the largest cities and the comfortable milieu of a small-town Main Street. They can also elect to do business in the privacy of their own home, converting once-useless space into a beehive of productive activity.

When these dreams evaporate, as too many do, the failure can often be traced back to a primary cause: the size and nature of the initial investment. Consider the case of Carol and Jerry Holt, who were convinced that they had discovered the formula that would forever solve their financial problems. It all sounded like a clever idea, selling high-quality imitation jewelry under a franchise known as Fabulous Fakes. For $18,000, they were promised, they would receive the necessary display and store fixtures, professional counseling for starting and operating the business, and a substantial inventory of the jewelry, which featured a type of imitation diamond called "cubic zirconia."

The Holts were assured that they could not possibly lose any money on the venture because they would get a full return on their investment just through discounts on future purchases to supplement their inventory as the merchandise was sold. Naively accepting these promises at face value, the Holts committed their total savings of $8,000 and convinced Jerry's parents to lend them $10,000 on a "can't-miss" basis.

Their investment purchased franchise rights in Towson, Maryland, convenient to their home. Sure enough, they quickly had a going business and began to sell their stocks of jewelry. Everything went smoothly for three months—until suddenly the requested shipments from the franchiser stopped. This was strange, since the Holts had been sending payments, including, in many cases, deposits from customers who wanted to order items that were out of stock.

Annoyed but not really worried, Jerry phoned Martin Baum, the Fabulous Fakes executive from whom they had purchased the franchise and who had made the promises. Unfortunately, he was "on vacation." A follow-up phone call a week later elicited nothing but the news that Baum was now "out of the country." His assistant or some other accountable person? They were always away too, or ill, or in perpetual conference.

"We never got an answer from anybody," said Carol Holt, describing the frustrations that finally led them to consult with an attorney. They were advised to close the shop before they got into trouble with customers, but by this time there was little business to terminate.

Ten months after he had promised the Holts the moon, Martin Baum was under investigation. He was later found guilty on four counts of fraud and four counts of selling unregistered franchises. Unfortunately for the Holts, they never received one cent of restitution.

Proceed with Caution

"For every headline-grabbing story about someone made a millionaire by McDonald's, Wendy's, or other franchisers," reported an editorial published in the *New York Times* in January 1986, "there are quieter stories about unknown people who have been made poor by unknown—and often nonexistent—franchise businesses. . . ."

As the *Times* warned, "In a nation enchanted with deregulation, the franchising laws may soon get looser even as fraud is flourishing." The state of Michigan, for example, which once had the most stringent franchising laws in the country, recently relaxed them. The step was taken to attract new business at a time when Michigan's economy was floundering, and it did indeed motivate hundreds of new franchisers to flock to the state. Most of the business that resulted has been legitimate and aboveboard. However, the deregulation did away with the state's customary review of sales literature and disclosure documents and made it more necessary than ever for would-be franchisees to investigate on their own before making down payments or signing agreements.

It has been reported that business opportunity swindles alone strip tens of thousands of investors of about half a billion dollars a year. Losses run from a few hundred dollars for an overpriced "start-up" inventory of consumer products to $12,000 or more for an "equity investment" in a franchise that is often nonexistent and at best very shaky. Some "distributorships" have a price tag of between $25,000 and $50,000. If the business is a bogus one or the merchandise is unmarketable—as was the case with three such operations closed down by the state of

New York in 1984—investors are out far more than just a little pocket money.

One prevalent scheme in the mid-1980s attracted about 350 investors to the Pacific Chemical Products Company in Ohio, which blatantly promised to provide at least 49 accounts—customers who were potential purchasers of large supplies of the product, cleaning solvents—to each franchisee. The company president and another officer were found guilty in United States District Court in Cleveland on charges of mail fraud. A federal grand jury charged that PCP was not an established business and was in no position to provide the sales accounts it had promised.

Investors lost an average of $6,000 apiece in the payment of useless fees that entitled them to become "affiliates" in the bogus venture. According to the district attorney who prosecuted the case, most victims could have avoided being duped had they taken the time to read the company's disclosure document closely. They would have learned that the company had previously been involved with fraudulent operations of a similar nature. What happens in cases like this, said the district attorney, is that "the perpetrators divert the victims' attention away from the paperwork," often pressuring them into hasty decisions and assuring participants that they will recoup their investment if the franchise does not work out to their satisfaction. The PCP fraud was the same old tune, simply played on a different instrument.

Even when you have invested in a legitimate franchise and are enjoying an ongoing, profitable business, you may find yourself at the mercy of swindlers who have devised other methods for parting you and your money. Take the case of Ben Wiskowski and his wife, who worked 12 to 14 hours a day for many years to establish and build an electrical supply business. The success of the enterprise eventually made it possible for Wiskowski to spend more time at job sites where he was installing equipment and for his wife to remain at home and raise their children. By this time, the firm had 15 employees and Wiskowski could delegate responsibilities, including the payment of invoices in a prompt and efficient manner to ensure a good credit rating.

Everything was proceeding well until he examined the books and was left with the distinct impression that the firm was paying far too much for certain types of office supplies. The reason surfaced quickly thereafter: Not all the invoices were authentic. A swindler was regularly submitting phony invoices to firms whose names he found in a business directory. Before Wiskowski discovered the fraud, his firm had paid out more than $7,000 to the con man.

But that amount, said the Chief Postal Inspector, was just a drop in the bucket. "Dollar losses on phony invoices run into the millions. . . . We have instances where a business has been sent 30 or 40 before someone got suspicious and started checking."

Investors not only have to be alert when they start a business but must remain relentlessly alert thereafter to avoid the ingenious traps that swindlers can devise.

Ten Tips for Prospective Franchisees

The romance, real or imagined, of going into business for oneself has captured the imagination of millions of Americans who are fed up with commuting, bored with nine-to-five office routines, or simply feel that the business has something new and fresh to offer. Unfortunately, the trend has also sparked the ingenuity and inventiveness of con artists who thrive wherever money is involved. The preposterous fact of the matter is that most of these swindlers are simply using variations on schemes that are as old as the Union itself.

To avoid falling victim to the ploys of these con artists, it is critical, above all, that you know your rights. Several states have laws that require franchisers to provide prospective purchasers with detailed information. In addition, a Federal Trade Commission rule requires that franchise opportunity promoters provide certain information to help you in your decision. Under the F T C rule, "A franchise or business opportunity seller must give you a detailed disclosure document at least 10 business days before you pay any money or legally commit yourself to a purchase." This document must provide 20 specific items of information about the business, including:

- the names and addresses of other purchasers,

- a fully audited financial statement,

- the credentials of the firm's key executives,

- the cost required to start and maintain the business,

- and the responsibilities you and the seller will have to each other once you go into the business.

The following ten tips from the New York State Attorney General's office are intended to help prospective franchise purchasers know what to look for and ask about before making any investment.

1. Make sure the seller of the franchise supplies you with a copy of the prospectus and that you read it carefully.

2. Consult with an attorney, an accountant, or another associate of proven knowledge and experience before paying any money or signing anything. Remember, you will be asked to pay a substantial sum of money, initially and during the course of the franchise relationship, and you will be committing yourself to a potentially long-term business relationship.

3. The experience of others is one of the most effective guides you can use to determine how you would do if you purchased a franchise. The prospectus should disclose the names and addresses of individuals currently operating franchises in the system. Contact them and ask them how their franchises are doing. Visit the franchised premises and observe the volume and type of business being done.
   Pay attention to the number of franchises terminated during the past three years—an unusually large number

may be a sign of danger. If there are no franchises, or very few, you will have no way of discovering from the experiences of others what you will be getting for your money.

4. Examine the financial statements in the prospectus with great care. An accountant or lawyer can analyze them and tell you of the franchiser's financial strengths and weaknesses. If the franchiser is financially weak, consider very carefully before you buy; he may be selling franchises as a way of raising cash just to stay in business.

5. Find out the number of hours and days per week you will be required to remain open and other rules the franchiser may have regarding the operation of the franchise. You may be unwilling or unable to work as many hours or days per week or per year as are required. Find out whether the franchiser has rules concerning closing for illness, death, or vacation; the number of employees you will be required to hire, if any; or anything else. You may find some of these rules too restrictive and burdensome. Some of these rules will be found in the prospectus, while others of a more detailed nature can be determined by questioning the franchise salesperson or broker with whom you are dealing.

6. Study carefully the estimate of initial expenses contained in the prospectus. If the estimate is too low, you may find yourself with insufficient cash to carry on until the business produces a cash flow.

7. In franchising, widespread customer recognition of a trade name is the equivalent of goodwill. An unknown name means that you and each member of the franchise system will have to develop goodwill and recognition. As such, you will not be buying goodwill, which is a leading feature of franchise operations. If the name is unfamiliar to you and your friends, you should ask yourself whether you are getting your money's worth in buying the franchise.

8. Examine the site selection process outlined in the prospectus, as the location of a franchise is very important. A poorly selected site will doom a franchise no matter how attractive its features. Determine what the franchiser will do to assist you in selecting an appropriate site and whether you will be able to change the site if it proves to be unsatisfactory. If the franchiser's participation in the site selection process appears to be perfunctory or if the franchiser offers no assistance, think twice about buying.

9. Training is one of the distinct advantages of franchising. It enables a franchise operator to acquire within a short time the skills an independent operator might take months or years to acquire. If the training described in the prospectus is not sufficiently detailed, ask about it. Also ask existing franchise operators about the training they received.

10. Know the franchise seller. A franchise agreement is only as good as the people behind it, regardless of how good it looks on paper. The prospectus gives certain information concerning the employment background of the principals of the franchiser and their litigation history. Check their employment background to see if they have been employed in franchising or a business related to the franchise being sold. Examine their litigation history. An excessive number of claims against them may mean that they have not been performing their agreements.

Five Warning Signs

Here are five danger signs to look for when you are considering making an investment in a franchise or other small-business venture. They were true in years past and will be just as valid in years to come.

1. *High-pressure sales tactics.* Be wary of sales pitches, whether from individuals or in ads, that urge you to get

in on the ground floor or to act at once. Shady promoters do not want you to take the time to read the small print, talk to others in the business, or visit facilities in person.

2. *Promises of exorbitant profits.* No honest business is built on quick, astronomical profits. A legitimate promoter will qualify his success stories and make it clear that profits depend on the diligence and capabilities of the individual, not on some surefire sales plan or a product so superior to all others that it cannot miss.

3. *Claims of no risk, or minimal risk.* Nothing in the world is riskier than going into business for yourself. No franchiser would ever assume the responsibility of underwriting franchisees who failed—unless he needed a huge tax loss. Assurances that "you can't go wrong in this business" are a sure tip that you are being conned. **ALERT!**

4. *Unjustified start-up fees.* If the job involves personal selling, there is no reason you should pay anything but a very modest fee to cover literature, enrollment, and basic training. If products are involved, check out their value and make sure you are not paying outlandish prices, perhaps for inferior goods.

5. *Evasive answers and lack of communication.* A promoter's failure to provide details and a disclosure statement or to respond directly to inquiries should diminish your enthusiasm for any franchise or business venture. He may be hiding facts that he does not want you to know. Even if he is honest, this kind of weak communication can quickly erode any business in which communication and cooperation are vital.

Chapter 3

INVESTING IN COMMODITIES AND FUTURES

ALERT!

Ask people outside the investment field what they think commodities trading is all about and at least one will provide a vivid description of men in shirtsleeves on a crowded Wall Street trading floor waving their arms furiously and shouting hoarsely as they buy and sell soybeans, corn, industrial metals, and other such staples essential to the well-being of the American consumer.

The picture, which once might have been quite accurate, is now outdated and only partly true to life. Today's markets in commodities and futures are open to a much broader range of participants than the specialists (then mostly men and only a handful of women) who used to ply their trade in the trading pits or arenas of major commodities exchanges. As an investor, you can now speculate on much more than what orange juice and pork bellies will cost two or three months from now. In addition to placing bets on produce from the surface of the earth and resources from beneath it, you can take a crack at estimating what foreign currency, interest rates, and inflation rates will be doing in the future.

Take the case of Marna and Peter Fowler who, until they were married three years ago, had never invested in anything more unorthodox than the common stocks of blue-chip companies. "One day, when we were pulling together our income tax records and reviewing the rather trivial amount we had made on the stock market," says Marna, "we decided that something was wrong. Although we were happy that we would be claiming a refund on our taxes, we also wished that we had been more adventuresome in the marketplace."

That was when, with the assistance of a Wall Street friend, they began to explore the areas of activity involved in futures markets and discovered that they could speculate on Treasury-bond futures by trying to anticipate the fluctuations in interest rates. Another alternative was to trade in stock-index futures and try to judge what the stock market would do over a period of several months. A third option was to invest in currency futures and speculate on the rise and fall of the dollar. They decided that, win or lose, it would be worth the excitement to set aside 20 percent of their investment money and try to out-guess the experts.

As their friend warned them from the beginning, the odds against success for amateurs were about ten to one. They would be treading on dangerous ground where they not only might lose their initial capital fast but also could be held accountable for much more if their speculation backfired. In the end, they made the decision to trade through a managed fund account, realizing that, in addition to being novices, they simply did not have the time or experience to make their own investment decisions. "Happily," reports Peter, "we had enough sense to place our chips in the hands of a manager whose fund had enjoyed a solid and well-documented track record over the past couple of years by pooling the contributions of many members and thus having sufficient resources. In one year, we made far more than we ever could have through more conservative investments."

Despite their initial success, the Fowlers made the decision not to increase their investment in futures, realizing full well that the next year's bottom line could be far less attractive, even with the help of professionals. They also resisted the temptation to go it on their own and speculate directly, rather than through a fund. "We were scared off a bit," admits Marna, "not only by some of the horror stories we had heard about scams and rip-offs in commodities but because we realized this field is risky even when you are dealing with an honest agent."

She was by no means being unduly apprehensive. As the North American Securities Administrators Association warned in a newsletter about commodities, "Unfortunately, as in most areas of investment where substantial profits can be made quickly, unscrupulous operators have set up shop and have taken millions of dollars a year from unsuspecting investors. In addition, they have been offering investment contracts or programs in such things as precious metals, which may *look* like futures contracts but are not traded on licensed futures exchanges. Predictably, these con men prey on individuals who probably should not be investing in commodities futures, who do not understand the transaction, and who can ill afford the potential losses." The newsletter might have added that it is not uncommon for *knowledgeable* investors also to be the victims of swindlers, who can be very clever and convincing.

Fruitless Futures

The unfortunate story of the Delancey brothers is a case in point. They had established a small business wholesaling detergents in the Philadelphia area and were convinced that they knew a good thing when they saw it. With increasing demand for exotic fruits and vegetables in stores ranging from mom-and-pop groceries to giant supermarkets, markups were far above normal for papaya, mangoes, and other produce from the Tropics and the Orient. So they were more than willing to listen to a "commodities expert from Hong Kong" who had come to the East Coast to sell futures contracts for a new strain of miniature banana to be shipped in quantity from Macao to New York in three months. Its price would skyrocket as the delivery date neared and the product was promoted to consumers.

The Delanceys knew little about futures contracts, even after talking with a commodities broker who traded largely in agricultural resources. It was a risky business, he informed them, and not for amateurs—not even for professionals unless they could monitor the market daily and keep abreast of a very volatile field of trading. Still, the brothers felt somewhat heady about their "inside information" and the fact that they were aware of continuing consumer demands. The new banana crop

could be a bonanza. So they handed a bank check for $10,000 to the Hong Kong trader as margin and made plans to realize their substantial profits when the time (not to mention the banana) was ripe.

Unfortunately, the deal was as rotten as fruit long past its prime. The Hong Kong Commodities Exchange had no knowledge of the proposed shipments. The "trader" who had smilingly taken their money turned out to be an expert in con games, not commodities, and was nowhere to be found. And the Delancey brothers ended up poorer but certainly a lot wiser for their $10,000 seminar in high finance.

Not everyone, of course, is going to be tempted by deals as exotic as tropical fruits. But many investors can be easily misled when they feel certain they are dealing with a reliable and well-established firm. The headlines and frequent newspaper accounts demonstrate otherwise. Consider this recent news release from the Associated Press under the headline FRAUD CHARGES ON FUTURES. "Seven businessmen were charged yesterday," said the account, "with bilking 1,200 investors out of $11 million by promising big profits on commodities futures traded by the Wall Street firm of Nelson, Ghun & Associates."

A federal grand jury in Manhattan charged the defendants with using high-pressure sales pitches and false claims to persuade "unsuspecting victims to part with their funds." People who fell for the scheme were lured by the firm's false assertion that it was using "computerized stop-loss trading techniques" that supposedly made it possible to detect adverse price fluctuations well in advance.

Promises, Promises

One of the problems faced by securities administrators and others attempting to monitor the commodities investment field is that many traders operate right on the borderline of the law, making regulatory action difficult. "Investors read or hear about huge returns in commodities and futures," says Andrew Berger of the law firm of Pollner, Mezan, Stolzberg, Berger & Glass, which has been involved with many cases in this field. "Naturally, they are tempted to risk their money for such gains. But the promoters are equally interested in making a lot of money fast and some will do so at almost any cost. In commodities, things move so fast and the client turnover is rapid and constant. So brokers are continuously looking for new clients. Another factor is that new types of instruments for investing are being devised all the time, which makes it difficult for brokers— let alone would-be investors—to understand just what they are getting involved with.

"Brokers become very defensive because of this lack of understanding of the details and thus shy away from trying to pass any information along to their customers. Nobody wants to take responsibility."

One reason lawyers handle so many cases involving commodities and futures, explains Berger, is that the risks are seldom disclosed. Customers who lose large sums of money therefore have a legitimate claim: They were not informed about the speculative nature of the trading at the time they committed their funds. Looking at such claims from the opposite side of the coin, brokers maintain large cash reserves to avoid litigation or fight any claims made by disgruntled customers. "Losing a lawsuit," says Berger, "is almost an open invitation to other claimants to sue."

Promoters who engage in questionable practices have few qualms about promising almost anything on the one hand and failing to mention the risks on the other. They know that people who invest smaller sums of money are not likely to take their case to court because the cost of doing so can be prohibitive. In one sorry case, a promoter ran up a printing bill of about $30,000 in the course of having a fancy brochure, showing him seated at a huge desk with an impressive backdrop of charts and maps, designed and printed. He used the brochure freely to advertise to prospective customers. But when he received the printing bill, he simply tore it up. "So sue me," he laughed, never having intended to pay and knowing that the printer would lose more than he could possibly gain if he took the matter to court.

Shady Traders

Every field of investment fraud has its classic case and most infamous villain. In commodities and futures trading, the person holding this "honor" is Marc Rich, who, in 1983, was described by *Time* magazine as "one of the shrewdest and most successful commodities traders in the world," with a personal fortune estimated at close to $1 billion.

Starting with some $5 million in seed money, Rich spawned a multicompany empire that traded sugar, aluminum, sulfur, oil, and other commodities. Among the rackets Rich created was one in which his company made a $71 million profit by illegally selling crude oil (some of it to nations hostile to the U.S.) at several times the government-regulated price. His wheelings and dealings were on such a gargantuan scale, however, that no one will ever unscramble the intricacies of his business dealings to learn how many people were taken in directly and indirectly by his schemes.

With 51 separate criminal charges filed against him—enough to earn prison sentences totaling 325 years—Rich fled the country in 1983, first to Switzerland and afterwards, reportedly, to Spain.

Though few of us have to worry about being victimized at this financial altitude, investors must sometimes be wary of dealing with even the most respected and prestigious names in the investment business. One of the top Wall Street firms was ordered recently by a federal court in Wisconsin to pay $28.2 million in damages to a foundation for having violated a trading agreement that resulted in an $8 million loss.

The foundation claimed that the firm "churned" its account—buying and selling securities indiscriminately—in a manner that ran up $2 million in commission fees. In addition, it asserted that the firm lost some $6 million in bad trades.

No matter how the case stood from a legal standpoint, it obviously exemplified the kind of lack of communication and understanding that can make trading in commodities a venture that no one should undertake without serious planning and watchful and responsible care.

In another case, in the spring of 1986, a well-known firm was shaken when the First Commodity Corporation of Boston became the first commodities firm to lose a suit brought under the Racketeer Influenced and Corrupt Organizations (RICO) Act of 1970. According to a July 1986 editorial in *Futures,* the magazine of commodities and options, "A federal jury in Wyoming found First Commodity and one of its brokers guilty of fraud and breach of fiduciary duties, and in violation of the Commodity Exchange Act. A jury ordered the firm and the broker to pay $69,802 actual damages, which was automatically tripled to $209,406. The jury also awarded $3 million in punitive damages."

The suit was filed against the firm and its broker by a former oil-field worker who accused them of using "high pressure and misleading tactics" to persuade him to invest more than $50,000 in commodities futures. Courtroom testimony documented a rather discouraging fact: First Commodity took 42 percent of the customer's investment in upfront fees before investing the balance in futures. Eventually, the firm sent the man a check for $1,388—representing little more than two and a half percent of his investment!

One of the problems faced by large investment houses, said an attorney who had just finished defending such a case, is that individual salespeople in affiliated offices down the line may not always conform to the letter and spirit of the law. They are tempted to make unrealistic promises or fail to disclose the risks if they see an opportunity to make a quick and easy profit. Hence, in many cases that are taken to court, officers of the firm will swear on the stand that they had no knowledge that a subordinate had violated the law. This kind of testimony is weak, however, in that the law makes managers responsible for supervising their agents.

In one such case, a prominent Philadelphia firm was indicted for failure to supervise employees effectively and properly. The branch manager defended himself by saying that he had no idea that any of his salespeople were engaging in illegal practices. "Firms simply must be *accountable,*" concluded the attorney, "particularly in a case like this when the manager was enjoying a hefty share of the profits."

The moral of all this is that you should take all reasonable means to assure yourself that the agent you deal with is honest. But remember, even if he is, commodities investing is risky under the best of circumstances, and there is virtually no limit on the commissions that can be charged to customers.

By and large, despite occasional violations by the major houses and the rash of publicity focusing on the indictments of traders who have used "inside" information illegally, the major threat to most investors comes from lesser-known firms that set up business with only one objective in mind: to take the customer's money and run. They are so adept at deceit that, as one former con man admitted, "Sometimes, when trying to convince a guy to part with his money, we began to believe that our own lies were truths!"

"The typical con artist lies well," says the Council of Better Business Bureaus (CBBB). "Some of the red flags to watch for include unsolicited, high-pressure phone calls; claims of confidential, inside information; urgent advice that you must act at once; promises of huge, quick profits; and assurances that your investment is absolutely at no risk and you will get your money back if you are dissatisfied."

The CBBB also warns against committing yourself to contracts that are tagged with phrases such as "fixed maturity," "deferred delivery," or "cash forward," which are not the types of contracts traded through regulated commodities exchanges. These terms are subtle ways of telling you that your cash is going to be tied up for a long, long time before you see any returns—if you ever do. When you see signs like these, your best course of action is to seek other investment opportunities that are safer and sounder.

Questions to Ask Before Investing

The greatest single risk—doing business with a dishonest salesperson or firm—can be avoided at the outset with little effort on your part. To play it safe, put your curiosity to work. Before dealing with any firm selling commodities, ask the following questions and make sure the answers are clear, understandable, and not hedged with "ifs," "maybes," and "buts." Evasive or incomplete answers should be regarded as warning signs.

- Is the firm a member of the National Futures Association or registered with the Commodity Futures Trading Commission or any other recognized regulatory agency? Pertinent licensing information and complaint history can be easily verified through these organizations, and if you feel you've been victimized, they can assist in arbitration of your claim.

- How long has the company been in business and who are its principals and officers?

- Are transactions executed through a regulated commodities exchange?

- Does the firm have a published disclosure statement or other written materials explaining the transactions and the risks?

- What percent of the initial investment will be allocated to commissions, fees, or other costs? (Since there are no specific limits on fees and commissions a trader can charge, it is important to know this in advance.)

- Where will these investment funds be held?

- Will the firm provide a copy of its financial statement?

- What independent references can be obtained from people who have dealt with the firm or know it?

ALERT!

The National Futures Association (NFA) has prepared a brochure entitled *Investor Swindles: How They Work and How to Avoid Them,* which is available free upon request. The association also offers brochures describing investors' rights and commodities investment. NFA is located at 200 West Madison Street, Suite 1600, Chicago, IL 60606, and provides two toll-free numbers: 800-572-9400 for Illinois residents and 800-621-3570 for callers from other states.

Chapter 4

PROBLEM-FREE FINANCIAL PLANNING

Never before in history have so many individuals, couples, families, and organizations invested their money in stocks, bonds, and other securities. For the most part, these investments have been financially rewarding, contributing to the general health of the economy and making it possible for countless millions of people to enjoy more comfortable lifestyles and provide security for the future. The most exciting drama on Wall Street has become the new-issue market, the process by which corporations of all sizes and types make it possible for the public to own shares in stocks and bonds in companies, individually and collectively. The annual volume in new issues has escalated to more than $135 billion, a figure that a generation ago would have seemed like something out of science fiction.

Much of the drama of new issues lies in the excitement of placing one's money in new and promising fields of endeavor, such as high-tech development, medical research, and computer innovations. Investing in a new company with no track record can be a gamble, resulting in either a substantial return or a resounding loss.

Yet this gigantic world of investments is only one of a sometimes puzzling multitude of financial opportunities available to any who want to play the money game. In addition to the public issues, which have to be processed through the federal Securities and Exchange Commission (SEC), there are about $50 billion worth of investments that are handled privately each year, often on little more than handshakes or through informal written papers. Most of these are stocks or some form of loan agreement in which the lender stands to profit if the project in question is successful. Many of the participants are not individuals but mutual-fund organizations, insurance companies, or limited partnerships. Although private investing is often the realm of small companies, giant corporations sometimes initiate private issues to underwrite special objectives.

Add to this dazzling financial array the world of government bonds, the recent trend toward buying options, and the little-understood fields of futures and commodities, and the average investor is likely to be confused and unsure about the best way to put available money to good use. It is no wonder that the financial planning industry has secured a solid position in the investment world and is growing at an explosive rate. Investors who are fortunate enough to have placed their future—or at least part of it—in the hands of capable and reliable financial planners have discovered that the relatively small expenses of fees and commissions can be negligible by comparison with the value of the counsel received and the financial actions taken as a result.

Financial planning services, which used to cater mainly to people of considerable wealth, are now available to millions of people of modest means who lack the time or experience to manage their income and assets properly. The number of financial planners in the two most widely recognized trade associations in the U.S. swelled from 15,000 in the early 1980s to about 40,000 by the middle of the decade and is still growing. They offer strategies for investing, cutting taxes, buying insurance, and taking other steps to build income or provide security for the future.

Millions of individuals and families have benefited from financial planning services, often earning profits from investments that they would never have dreamed of getting into without professional counsel. Others, however, have not only paid good money for bad advice but have gotten badly burned in the process. For the sad fact of the matter is that there are some 200,000 people who have hung up their shingles as "financial planners," many of whom are fortune hunters whose only objective is to use their customers as stepping-stones to self-enrichment. Despite the booming activity in this field and an estimate that 35 million American households could be customers for financial plans, the business is very loosely regulated and only a small percentage of the so-called experts are registered with the SEC.

One survey of consumer complaints and enforcement actions in 20 states revealed that fraud and abuse in the financial planning field was totaling more than $30 million a year in these areas alone. Some of the problems stemmed from inexperience and mismanagement, but a large percentage of the "financial planners" involved in these losses were outright swindlers who engaged in various scams and rip-offs with no intention of planning anything besides making themselves a fast buck.

Variations on a Scheme

It is only too easy to find yourselves in the hands of a professional charlatan if you fail to check out the honesty and reliability of the person you intend to deal with. Take the case of James and Laura, an average American couple of moderate means who could well have benefited from sound counseling. As he approached normal retirement age, James decided that he had acquired enough savings over the years and would have a large-enough pension for it to make sense to engage the services of a professional financial planner. Laura agreed. In fact, she had just received a letter and some printed matter in the mail from an investment counseling firm in Chicago, describing its valuable services to people who, "with the constant demands on one's time these days, are too busy to manage their money with the care and foresight necessary." Furthermore, explained the letter, "We will be happy to evaluate your needs and make an initial recommendation at no cost or commitment to you."

Deciding that they had little to lose and much to gain, James and Laura sent the executive vice president of the firm a candid list of their assets, income, and future expectations. The response was enthusiastic and immediate, a written proposal that was a bit hard to follow but was filled with glowing promises. In essence, it reported that the couple's net worth was such that they were not even beginning to develop the monetary potential they should already be enjoying. For a very small consulting fee, a mere $1,800, the firm would draw up a financial plan that would "help money make money" and, of course, that would quickly cover the modest cost of putting the plan into action.

The $1,800 did, indeed, seem to be well spent when James received a personal "Evaluation Report" and recommendations for "activating" his finances by transferring some of the funds into income-producing investments. It so happened, said the executive vice president in a follow-up phone call, that he could provide very quick evidence of the kind of prosperity he could generate if James would sell one of his passive assets and let the firm place the proceeds, about $5,000, in a little-known but promising high-tech stock venture. Assured that there was no risk and that the firm was anxious to prove its capabilities to "people like you who will be our blue-chip customers of the future," James went along with the advice of his newly acquired financial planner.

The outcome is easy to guess. The surefire investment was a no-risk one all right—for the firm! James and Laura never saw a penny of profit and lost all of the initial fee and most of the $5,000. When James tried to track down the executive vice president in his Chicago lair, he discovered that the fancy address was nothing but a tiny back office rented on a month-to-month basis for use as a mailbox and phone booth. He might easily have saved himself a financial loss, not to mention considerable emotional stress and embarrassment, had he checked out the financial planner in advance.

There are so many variations in the field of bogus financial planning that investors have to be alert in order to avoid getting taken. A recent report in *Barron's* magazine, for example, included the following thumbnail examples of what was described as "an epidemic of fraud and abuses arising from the underside of the financial planning industry."

- Maryland authorities froze the assets of a two-man investment counseling firm that promised to return 30 percent in just 90 days on funds deposited by its clients. Although a total of more than $2.5 million had been taken in, only one-fourth of the money was recovered. Even at that, the unhappy investors were fortunate to get back 25 cents on the dollar.

- A "financial planner" in Phoenix concocted a phony investment club whose members were supposedly going to profit from the sale of pelts and meat from a breed of "super" rabbit. The 40 members who signed up lost almost all of their investment, averaging about $27,000 apiece.

- In Oregon, investigators took action against a financial planner who had already swindled $2.8 million from his customers. His plan of action was to collect $1,500 from each client, for which fee he promised to draw up investment plans. Instead, he did nothing but use the contacts to further another scam: an abusive tax shelter.

- Georgia securities officials prosecuted a financial planner who allegedly converted his clients' cash into worthless certificates of deposit.

- A New Jersey financial planner lured his customers by promising them a 14 percent return on a "special money market account." Instead, he lost most of their money in a shaky real-estate deal that went sour.

Financial Planner:
The Facts behind the Phrase

Just what *is* a legitimate financial planner and what does he do to help clients? The answer is not all that simple. "We no longer live in simple times," says Lawrence B. Eichler, a partner in a financial consulting firm. "Instead, we have the confusion and chaos produced by an expanding economy and increasing deregulation of the financial services industries. Each group of counselors/advisers is trying to grab a bigger slice of the financial services pie. Stock brokerage houses sell real estate, insurance companies now own stock brokerage houses, banks sell insurance policies, and CPAs do appraisal work. And capitalizing on the public's desire for surefooted investment decisions, more and more of these hybrid professionals have styled themselves 'financial planners'—experts who can develop an overall financial strategy custom-tailored to your personal needs."

A financial planner can be almost anyone. Many brokers, attorneys, accountants, and insurance companies now promote their services in conjunction with the concept of financial planning. The best financial planners will be knowledgeable about law, accounting, taxation, and insurance, in addition to stocks, bonds, limited partnerships, and other investment subjects. They can advise you regarding your will, and on ways to structure your estate, lower your taxes, provide for your insurance needs, and plan for your retirement.

It is, however, important to realize that, unlike the brokerage industry, the field of financial planning is still largely unregulated. A plumber or butcher could start up a part-time financial planning service without completing any academic program, passing any certifying exam, or having any training in the field.

Concerned about the nature, numbers, and varied experience of newcomers in their field, the financial planning trade associations face a double-edged challenge. On the one hand, some want to put teeth into actions that will discourage the inept and the shady from doing business. On the other hand, some want to keep government regulation and restriction at a minimum so that their members can go about their business freely and effectively. The Institute of Certified Financial Planners imposes educational standards for membership and requires its members to hold certificates from the College for Financial Planning. The International Association for Financial Planning accepts only those members who agree to abide by its professional code of ethics. The newest trade organization, the National Association of Personal Financial Advisors, also has stringent requirements but limits its members to planners who charge set fees for their consulting services and do not derive commissions from any of the investments that their clients might purchase.

From the standpoint of federal and state regulations, however, until recently nothing has required people who want to offer their services in financial planning to know anything specific about the business, and the regulations are still somewhat loose. Unlike CPAs or attorneys, who must pass stiff examinations before they can be licensed, financial planners need do little more than announce their intentions and start soliciting clients.

Because of this situation, many conscientious planners voluntarily enroll in courses at the American College in Bryn Mawr, Pennsylvania, or the College for Financial Planning in Denver in order to earn documentary evidence of their abilities. After passing examinations in related subjects such as insurance, investments, tax law, and estate planning, and providing certain professional credentials, they are awarded certificates conferring on them such titles as CFP ("Certified Financial Planner"). Because of the increasing demand, more than a dozen colleges and universities now offer some form of certificate or degree programs that bolster their students' standing as financial planners.

According to existing law (the Investment Advisers Act of 1940), financial planners and anyone else who offers, for a fee, to furnish advice on the purchase and sale of securities are considered to be *investment advisers* and are thus required to register with the SEC. In addition, they must comply with rules that regulate advertising and record-keeping and provide disclosure statements to prospective customers.

Although these advisers are required to file an application for licensing that discloses any criminal background they might have, there are no educational or testing requirements to become registered with the SEC as an investment adviser. Some states have recently adopted legislation requiring investment advisers to be licensed on the state level and, in some cases, to meet certain testing requirements.

Unfortunately, some financial planners do not register with the SEC, which makes the job of regulation and supervision much more difficult. Others avoid regulation by not charging a counseling fee but promoting other services from which they can turn a profit. Many planners are little more than glorified salespersons whose ultimate objective is to sign you up for life insurance, sell you mutual funds, or peddle municipal bonds.

"Few planners merely plan," said an editorial in *U.S. News & World Report.*

"For most, it's a sideline to the insurance, brokerage, banking, or other businesses." In such cases, it could hardly be claimed that you are being victimized by a scam. Yet your ultimate goals may become unnecessarily befogged or diverted.

According to an article in *Consumers Research* magazine, "A good financial planner should help you to develop a budget and an investment strategy most suitable to you." Or, in the words of a *Money* magazine article, "Insist that your planner demonstrate how taking his suggestions will improve your bottom line—not his."

Fees and Other Factors

There are basically three types of financial planners. First, there are those who sell only financial plans and then refer their clients to others who sell financial products, such as stocks, mutual funds, insurance plans, bonds, real-estate partnerships, and other investments. Second, there are those who charge for their counsel and also receive commissions for selling some or all of the investments they recommend. Third, there are those who make no overall charge for the plans but earn commissions on the financial products they recommend in the plans.

How much does financial planning cost? There is no "typical" budget figure. Fees can be fixed, ranging from $100 to $10,000. Or they can be charged on a time-and-work basis, at rates from $50 to $300 or more an hour. Some planners have modest initial fees but charge extra for writing a plan, implementing it, or providing an annual review. Other counselors use a percentage formula, based on the size of each client's earned income or total investment under the plan.

Preparing to meet with a financial planner to further your objectives is not always easy. As Lisa Berger, a business journalist, comments, "Financial planning can be a profitable but rigorous experience. It means digging into your financial past and pulling out records and receipts. You can't walk into a planner's office and dump a shoebox full of old receipts and cancelled checks on the desk and expect an instant blueprint. You first have to organize your records, round up documents, such as wills and stock certificates, and make decisions about your financial goals. Once you have done your homework, a planner should help you come up with a game plan that will lead to financial security."

Shopping around for a reliable financial planner is not as difficult as it might seem. A good place to start is through people who you know have enjoyed satisfactory relationships with their own planners over a period of several years. Ask for recommendations from people you already know or deal with in the financial community, such as brokers, bankers, your accountant, or someone who has handled a family estate. You can also obtain the names of planners in your area through the trade associations mentioned earlier.

The International Association for Financial Planning suggests that you obtain answers to the following questions from whatever candidates you are seriously considering.

- What educational and financial experience does the planner have and in what professional organizations does he hold membership? (It's a good idea to verify his answer by calling the organization. In asking about his educational background, you can look for several degrees. One is certified financial planner. To attain this degree, a person must first complete a two-year financial planning course. Chartered financial consultant and certified life underwriter are other titles to look for. Each designation has different requirements, so ask for a specific explanation of the title and the address of the educational institution so that you can verify what you are told.)

- If the planner claims to be an investment adviser, check with your state securities commission and with the regional SEC office nearest you to determine whether he is duly licensed.

- What specific experience does he have in the areas you are most concerned about, as well as in subject fields that you would like to explore?

- Will he be not only compatible with you but sympathetic to the needs of your particular income bracket?

- What specific services does he offer, what will they cost, and how will remuneration be made? (These data should be obtained in writing.)

ALERT!

- Will he provide a *written* summary, document his recommendations, and review your progress periodically?

- Does he offer ready access to other financial experts, as well as reliable sources of information?

If you feel that the procedure is all too complicated and involved, take heart from the case of former teacher Rickie Cowin, who, at the age of 35, took her small pension and went into real estate. Admitting that her financial knowledge "bordered on the nonexistent," she located a reliable investment adviser who demanded no advance fee but worked on a commission basis. He placed her funds, about $6,000, in a short-term certificate of deposit (CD) as a starter, helping her to read and understand the bank statements when they arrived in the mail. Even this small financial move was a traumatic experience for Rickie.

"I'm very conservative," she said. "I would sleep with my money in my hands if I could."

As her income grew and the CD matured, she accepted the planner's advice to invest in public utilities, which also offered a certain tax advantage now that she had climbed to a higher bracket. "We always need gas and electricity," she assured herself, trying to overcome innate doubts about venturing over her head in the investment sea. As she explained, her family had reared her in a world where money was supposed to be placed in the safety of the most dependable bank in town, behind imposing bulwarks that you could actually *see*.

Over a six-year period, Cowin came to trust her planner's advice, as well as to have more confidence in her own decision-making. After she realized a 160 percent return on her utility stocks and discussed ways of broadening her investment plan, she closed what was left of her savings account in favor of a cash-management account. "Saying goodbye to the bank was a big deal for me," she admitted, confirming the fact that her attitude had changed greatly as a result of establishing realistic goals and that, in the process, she had finally recognized the advantages of financial planning.

Financial planning is certainly not for everyone. And putting yourself in the hands of an inept or unethical financial planner is worse than having no plan at all. But it makes sense to undertake a serious study of what you *could* do with your assets, both to make profits and to ensure a more secure future. If you study your options and investigate thoroughly before making any commitments, you are almost certain to come out ahead of the game.

Guidelines for a Sound Financial Plan

Before you can expect a competent financial planner to be able to help, you must take the following steps.

- Compile all the data you can—the more specific the better—concerning your income, bank accounts, real estate, income taxes, wills, loans, budgets, and other related financial matters.

- Identify your goals and describe your objectives, whether as an individual, a couple, or a family.

- List any major changes, past, present, and future, that could modify your objectives. These include happenings such as births, marriages, retirement, change of jobs, and relocation.

- Identify financial crises and trouble spots such as mounting debts, tax increases, or chronic illness.

- Make a list of other professionals who assist you, or who have in the past, including attorneys, accountants, brokers, and bankers.

No matter what type of financial planner you elect to use, you should expect to obtain the following services.

- A clearly written plan, in language you can understand, containing a balance sheet of profits vs liabilities and an explanation of goals.

ALERT!

- Disclosure of the amount of risk estimated in pursuit of the objectives.

- Specific suggestions for improving your personal cash management.

- Projections for shifts in the rate of interest, inflation, and other situations that will affect your plan in the future.

- Options and alternatives, providing a range of investment choices with a list of the advantages and disadvantages of each course of action.

- A plan for liquidity in the event of emergencies, outlining ways to obtain reserve cash with the least amount of disruption and cost.

- Suggested sources of advice from other professionals, particularly if you do not have a regular accountant, attorney, insurance agent, or stockbroker.

- A proposed schedule for monitoring your financial plan and reviewing its progress and objectives periodically.

Chapter 5

FOOL'S GOLD AND OTHER "VALUABLES"

ALERT!

The proposal that Mrs. J. Harold Templeton, a well-to-do widow, received in the mail was tempting. A silver dealer in Colorado was actively buying up family collections of silver at prices much higher than the current market value. Did Mrs. Templeton have any silver that she was interested in selling, or did she know of others who might be willing to part with items that they no longer cared to store and insure?

Mrs. Templeton did not, but her eye was caught by a small, unobtrusive leaflet describing the Colorado firm's "silver investment program" and requesting interested prospects to send for details "under no obligation." Curious, Mrs. Templeton filled out the coupon attached.

The response was a phone call from a Mr. Leonard in Denver, who said that he represented the dealer and that he was phoning rather than using the mails because "Rather exciting events have been shaping up that would-be investors should know about while the opportunity is still ripe."

His comments, though a bit charged with high-pressure terminology, were convincing. The reason he and his partners were buying as much silver as they could at above-market prices was that they had some remarkable and thoroughly reliable inside information. Brand-new computer technology originating in IBM labs was calling for pure-silver circuit systems. When millions of the new computers started coming off the assembly line, the demand for silver would skyrocket, so much so that "spot" prices would probably double within the following few months.

Some of the dealer's valued customers were getting in on this expected bonanza. How? By placing orders for silver at current low prices and then receiving their shipments of the precious metal in two or three months, by which time the price of silver would be much, much higher than what they had paid. Although Mrs. Templeton was not yet a customer, her name was well known and Mr. Leonard had been authorized to include her in the offer as someone the Colorado firm would be honored to have as a customer.

Fortunately—at least as far as Mrs. Templeton was concerned—the story had a happy ending when her sense of curiosity prompted her to phone a close friend who was an officer at IBM. The "silver circuit" story was pure fiction and, even if it had been true, would have had little effect upon the price of silver. The silver dealer in Colorado turned out to be an old hand at gold and silver swindles and was already folding up shop and moving to a new location and a new con game.

Cooling Gold Fever

"Even if you've been inoculated with a healthy dose of investment caution, it's easy to catch gold fever these days," commented an editorial in *Business Week* in late 1986, reporting that the price of the precious metal had risen about one-third in less than a year. Adding to the glamour of this form of investment was the appearance on the market of the American Eagle, the first new U.S. gold coin issued in 50 years, and the fact that many professional analysts were once again recommending that their customers consider gold in well-diversified portfolios in quantities ranging as high as 15 percent of their total holdings.

The gold market can be extremely volatile. The price of gold fluctuates in response to a wide variety of factors, including, among others, supply and demand, inflationary expectations, and government economic policies. As mentioned in chapter 1, would-be buyers were turned off emphatically by the sad case of the International Gold Bullion Exchange and the illegal wheelings and dealings of the Alderdice brothers. But investor interest rebounded when gold's tarnish faded and the metal started to come back into the spotlight in a more positive way.

If you want to invest in gold or other precious metals, make sure that you are dealing with a reputable dealer. There are a number of ways in which you can invest in gold. If you are taken with the idea of owning gold as an actual, physical commodity, you can purchase gold bullion, ranging in amounts from wafers weighing less than an ounce to bricks weighing as much as 20 or 25 pounds. What you then have in your possession is virtually pure gold, for which you pay the current market price, plus a premium that may range from less than two percent to as much as seven percent.

Most new investors favor coins as the most practical—and certainly the most aesthetically pleasing—way of investing in gold. The types of coins referred to here are those that are priced on their gold content alone, plus a premium that may range from four to eight percent. The most popular foreign coins (following the ban in the United States on imports of the South African Krugerrand) are the Canadian Maple Leaf, the Austrian Corona, and the Mexican 50-Peso. These can be purchased easily through banks and brokers.

Do not confuse these coins with the *numismatic* variety, whose prices, like those of philatelic stamps, are based on other factors in addition to the amount of gold they contain, such as rarity, physical condition, age, and historical value. Investing in numismatic coins is highly specialized, and it would require an entire book just to cover the basics, let alone the subtleties and technicalities of collecting. You should know, however— if this is a field of investment that might interest you more than precious metals per se—that there has been some progress in recent years in developing standards for the valuation of numismatic coins.

One development, for example, has been the creation of a dealer network, the Professional Coin Grading Service (PCGS), which is made up of more than 50 dealers nationwide.

Thus far, PCGS has graded more than 200,000 different coins of the types that are valued by collectors. These include such collectibles as gold coins, silver dollars, commemorative half dollars, and the so-called "type" coins, which are obsolete designs that are no longer being minted. Grading involves a standardized system whereby coins can be valued on a scale ranging from Mint State 0 to the top grade, Mint State 70. Various criteria for selecting a grade are used, including, for example, a coin's wear and tear—nicks, scratches, luster, color, and clarity of imprinting.

Grading is not infallible by any means, but it does provide several advantages for people who want to collect or invest in rare coins. For one thing, grading provides a measure of protection to both buyers and sellers who deal with PCGS members. Furthermore, the existence of a uniform grading system ensures a more liquid market in numismatic coins. That means that investors in rare coins can sell their coins more quickly and efficiently than in the past. Yet scams exist in numismatics, too. Dealers have been known to misgrade, misrepresent rarity, or charge exorbitant prices for coins.

The process of buying gold sounds simple and direct. What better, more tangible asset could one possibly have? However, you should realize that if you actually want to take possession of the metal, any profit you make on its sale will be reduced by sales taxes, fees, delivery charges, and other transaction-related fees. There is also the question of safe storage and the high cost of insurance. Also, when the market for other forms of investments seems attractive (or you need the cash), you cannot negotiate a sale until you have had your cache of bullion assayed. This procedure takes a week or more and can cost as much as one dollar for each ounce of gold you wish to sell.

Another way to invest in gold is through the purchase of gold certificates, which can be acquired through many firms that deal in precious metals. These documents certify that you own the amount of gold stated on their face and that it must be delivered to you or to whomever you designate at any time, on demand. If you hold certificates, which are available not only for gold but for silver, platinum, or any other precious metals, you will be required to pay annual storage charges to your bank or broker. Such charges can vary from approximately two percent for small amounts to less than one percent for large holdings.

The primary advantages to purchasing precious-metal certificates, as opposed to taking delivery of the metal, are the reduction of certain transaction-related expenses, the elimination of the necessity of finding your own storage place for the metal, and the greater ease of resale.

You should also realize that you can invest in a variety of mutual funds whose portfolios are oriented toward gold and other precious metals. These funds offer a variety of investment approaches, as well as geographical emphasis. Many, for example, own stock in South African gold mining concerns, while others concentrate on North American companies or offer a mix that includes Australian concerns.

Pitches and Pitfalls

No matter how small an amount of money you commit to your initial plunge into precious metals, be cautious and make certain that you are not placing yourself in the hands of a disreputable trader. As is the case in any financial dealing in which you have to rely on the other fellow's integrity and honesty, you should never rush so fast to get in on a "sure thing" that you fail to investigate before investing. The lure of gold is one of the age-old allies of the swindler, the con man, and the shady operator. For every honest program for making money in the precious-metals market, there are at least two that are either outright scams or are schemes heavily slanted in favor of the promoter. Be especially cautious if a salesperson (or sales literature) promises that you will enjoy huge returns on your investment, that you can expect quick profits, or that there is "no risk." Remember, no matter what anyone tells you, investing in gold or other precious metals is always a risky business. Bear in mind, too, that the market is highly volatile and can move up or down at surprising speed.

Precious-metals scams and swindles seem to run in cycles, surfacing most dramatically when such metals are regularly in the news. Be wary when you see a rash of advertising campaigns in newspapers or on television that try to attract purchasers of gold coins, silver coins, or bullion at or below spot prices. Unfortunately, many of the firms that make such offerings can launch a business and stay in it without being subject to any state or federal licensing and with few restrictions against high-pressure sales tactics. Even when unscrupulous firms exceed legal boundaries and are charged or indicted by law-enforcement agencies, they often manage to stay in business and bilk customers for many months thereafter before they are finally closed down.

Such was the case, for example, with the International Gold Bullion Exchange (IGBE), which continued its operations long after the state of Florida initially tried to impose trading curbs and the press was citing the firm for shady practices. IGBE's stock-in-trade—common to most precious-metals schemes—was to smooth-talk investors into accepting "deferred delivery," a sneaky way of saying that they would not catch a glimpse of their purchase for months, if ever.

One type of deferred-delivery scam follows this pattern: A firm offers the purchaser a specific precious metal at a price that is below the spot price offered by legitimate firms, and offers to waive the customary dealer's commission. The customer then pays up front for his purchase of bullion or coins, at the same time agreeing that he will not receive the delivery of his order for an extended period, often for as long as four months. When the delivery date nears, the hopeful purchaser is then confronted with another offer that seems too good to turn down: He can receive a two or three percent return on his money *per month* if he will again defer taking delivery of his silver or gold. Upon receiving checks for this promised "bonus," few customers balk at the idea and demand complete delivery.

In the case of the IGBE swindle, a large percentage of some 25,000 investors were conned into leaving their gold with the firm. An astonishing number were even persuaded to ship bullion and coins they had purchased from legitimate dealers to the promoters of the scheme for "safekeeping and additional investment." When the swindlers were indicted and the firm went bankrupt, these victims lost everything.

All That Glitters . . .

Devastating to millions of small investors, and almost impossible for the law-enforcement agencies to prosecute, is the steady market in fake and low-quality "precious gems." These masquerading little devils seldom send individual investors to the poorhouse or trigger cases of major bankruptcy, yet in sum total they are responsible for millions upon millions of dollars of fraud perpetrated on the American public.

Precious and semiprecious gemstones are heavily promoted by less-than-ethical firms that count on the fact that there are millions of prospects out there who still believe they can get something for nothing. Taking full advantage of this weakness in human nature, high-pressure operators, many of whom have been based in Florida and California, push thousands of low-grade rubies, sapphires, and garnets on unsuspecting investors across the nation who are conned into thinking they are dealing with reputable jewelers. Here are some actual cases of investors who were bilked during one wave of junk-gem promotions.

- An architect in Nevada paid $45,000 for a "portfolio" of six sapphires and six rubies touted as a "sacrifice by a jeweler facing bankruptcy." The only sacrifice was on the part of the buyer. When he placed the gems in the hands of his local jeweler for appraisal for insurance purposes, he learned that the total value of the dozen stones was $4,500 or less.

- A Florida real-estate broker traded a diamond ring worth $1,000 and an additional $1,600 in cash for six "unique and very valuable garnets" offered by a fast-talking gem promoter. The garnets were later evaluated as being worth $45 maximum at wholesale.

- An Ohio doctor withdrew $18,000 from a savings account he had started for his son's college education in order to double its value through the purchase of five sapphires that had "just come from an estate being liquidated quickly in order to pay off family debts." In his haste to snag a bargain, he did not consult a gem dealer until after making his purchase. He was understandably shocked to learn that he could have bought five similar sapphires from his local jeweler for less than $1,200.

- A consulting engineer in North Dakota paid an itinerant gem dealer $2,000 for a 10-carat parcel of garnets that were promoted as a "one-of-a-kind investment." To his chagrin, he soon learned that he had purchased a sack of low-value industrial stones and that, in effect, he had been short-changed by about $1,950.

According to C. R. ("Cap") Beesley, president of Gemline Recovery Service (GRS), Americans spend upwards of $100 million each year on "meretricious baubles" for which they pay outlandish prices, often after having been talked into believing that they are making sound investments. GRS, which is the consumer counseling division of American Gemological Laboratories in New York City, has been investigating cases of fraud like the ones cited above since it was founded in 1982, and it reports that such swindles are on the increase. According to Beesley, it is a sad fact that junk-gem dealers and boiler-room operators now outnumber legitimate dealers and jewelers, evidence that American consumers are more gullible than ever when it comes to investing.

Promoters of junk gems are most active when there is any kind of turmoil in markets dealing in securities, commodities, or precious metals. That is when inexperienced investors are likely to be scared away from conventional types of investments and become easy marks for the hustlers who come up with alternate plans for the placement of money. "It goes without saying," reports Jean-Frances Moyerson, an investment banker who publishes a gemstone report, "that unscrupulous sellers will try to capitalize on this kind of tumultuous market. There is so much more interest in colored stones now and they lend themselves far more readily to deception than diamonds."

The promotional patterns of these swindlers reveal that they very cleverly move from one type of stone to another whenever prospective buyers are scared off by bad publicity involving specific cases of deceit. "As soon as investors get wise to the shoddy quality of the sapphires and garnets they are buying," explains Donald Palmieri, a gem appraiser and broker in Pittsburgh, "the boiler rooms will move on to some other gem and prices will tumble. These are phony markets, but only the phonies know it."

As Beesley points out, thousands upon thousands of gems that can be purchased for a few dollars a carat at any legitimate gem and mineral show are sold over the phone for hundreds of dollars per carat. Yet, even though this price discrepancy is an "iron-clad tip-off to fraud," there is often very little that irate purchasers can do when they find out they have been gypped.

"The wheels of justice grind very slowly when it comes to gem frauds," says Beesley. "You've got to sell a lot of Brooklyn Bridges before the authorities will sit up and take notice. Compared with, say, oil and gas ripoffs, gem scams seem like penny-ante stuff."

Inexperienced investors in gems plunge into a netherworld where they have very little recourse to the law when they feel they have been duped. "Attempts to treat gem deals like securities transactions and to prosecute gem investment firms under securities laws have been rebuffed repeatedly by both federal and state courts," reports David Federman, editor of the trade newsletter *Precious Stones.* "About the only federal laws that apply are the general fraud statutes enforced by the Federal Trade Commission (FTC), and fraud is hard to prove. In fact, since precious stones came into vogue as investments in the late 1970s, the FTC has been able to obtain from the courts just *two* consent orders against gem investment companies."

Why do so many otherwise intelligent investors keep falling victim to high-pressure sales pitches and exorbitant claims touted in slick mailing pieces?

Basically, explains Beesley, they get hooked before they realize it, because they think they are dealing with bona fide investment counselors who are advising clients to consider gems as the investment opportunity of the moment. They fail to realize that the person on the other end of the line is a skilled actor, not a skilled analyst. Often, boiler-room operators are simply reading from prepared scripts and have as little knowledge about gems as they have about the moon.

Unlike investors in securities and commodities, who can check their newspapers on a daily basis for updated price quotes, those who put their money in precious or semiprecious stones frequently find themselves in the dark as to the current value of their investments. Gems are one of the trickiest of investment purchases, explains Beesley. They have to be selected on the basis of quality, color, rarity, and value—along with other criteria that require extensive professional knowledge to sort out and evaluate. Since very few investors possess this kind of knowledge, they simply have to rely on their sources and trust their judgment.

Cap Beesley is understandably disturbed by the bad press gemologists receive whenever cases of fraud come to light. "That's what really hurts about all this," he says. "Gems can make an excellent investment. It's just a matter of using some sense when shopping for them. But investors don't make the effort. Hell, they use more caution when buying a $30 toaster than a $3,000 gem!"

Before You Invest
In Precious Metals . . .

Consider the following words of advice from those who have reputable standings in this field of investment.

- Question the reputation of any firm that offers to sell you precious metals at "below spot prices" and undercut the market. *ALERT!*

- Look suspiciously on a plan whereby a dealer promises you "rebates" as a sign of good faith that he is actually holding metals for you.

- Be wary of any hesitation about delivering your metals promptly upon request.

- Make certain that your investment will be kept separate from the firm's operating funds.

- Pay for your purchase through arrangement with your bank for a bank draft, which will not be released until the purchase is in hand.

- Demand evidence when purchasing coins or bullion that there is no chance of counterfeiting by the supplier.

- Check the legitimacy of the dealer and do not be timid about requesting references.

- Make certain that warehouse receipts and gold or silver certificates are valid.

- **ALERT!** Bear in mind that, even under the best of circumstances, when dealing with scrupulously honest dealers, the precious-metals market is a volatile one and trading in it can be risky.

- Take into consideration the fact that what you buy at retail price you often have to sell at wholesale, with the market against you.

- Be aware that deferred-delivery contracts for precious metals are not government-regulated.

- Unless you are highly knowledgeable, avoid offers to invest in "strategic" metals like titanium and cobalt.

- Take your time and reject all urges to rush into an investment "before it is too late." If you have any questions or suspicions about a metals dealer, contact your state's Securities Division or the Consumer Fraud Division of your state's Attorney General's office *before* you invest.

Before You Invest in Gems . . .

Make certain that you have covered the following points.

- Check the American Gem Society or American Gemological Laboratories to ascertain the reliability and standing of the firm making the offer.

66

- Insist that your purchase be subject to professional appraisal and a money-back guarantee if there is any discrepancy between the purchase price and the evaluation.

- Avoid any pressure to make a quick purchase at a "low, low price."

- Look askance at claims that the price is a sacrifice because of bankruptcy proceedings or the need to close out an estate quickly.

- Ask for business references, as well as the names of satisfied buyers.

ALERT!

- Demand prior documentation, including the exact color and nature of each gem, its place of origin, its category, and its condition.

- If you still have questions or doubts, hire a gemologist to represent you.

Chapter 6
LURE OF THE LAND

ALERT!

Few indeed are the individuals, couples, or families who have not received by mail or phone the "news" that they have just won free drinks, a gourmet dinner, and a chance to meet with congenial people and see a film portraying the wonderful new way of life they can enjoy at one of America's finest recreation communities of tomorrow. Many invitations imply, too, that the "winners" can enjoy a free weekend at the dream community in question, basking by the Olympic-sized pool, paddling across the crystal-clear waters of the lake, playing a round of golf on the championship course, and sampling the charms of a candlelight dinner at a cherished old farmhouse converted into a community inn.

Most Americans with substantial sums to invest in real estate have long since considered themselves too sophisticated to fall for the puffery and promises of this kind of promotion. They know full well that the evening or weekend will be nothing short of a sometimes distasteful, always high-pressure promotion to buy property. But today, the promotions have become more subtle and in many cases the stakes have become considerably higher than they used to be. Enterprising promoters are exploiting vulnerable markets in four major types of real estate: raw land, recreation sites, second homes, and retirement residences. While much of the marketing is honest and legitimate, unfortunately the rest ranges from questionable misrepresentation to outright fraud.

Mute evidence of the latter was a ghost town that, until recently, stretched along Route I-30 outside Dallas, Texas. "Rows of unfinished condominiums border the freeway, roughly 2,500 units in all," reported *Forbes* magazine in mid-1985. "Chimneys are falling, windows are broken, tar paper peels from uncovered walls. . . ."

As is easy to imagine, the development was fraudulent from the start, luring investors with promises of huge returns through the purchase and sale of condominiums. The story had a familiar ring to investigators who found themselves hot on the trail of a major scam. But wait a minute! There was a unique twist to this tale, a gimmick not previously encountered in the annals of real-estate schemes. The promoters had engineered their financial sleight of hand so adroitly that they not only were getting away with the money but were leaving many of the early investors, who had made $20,000 or more without putting up a dime, in the hot seat, facing indictment and astronomical debts.

According to the assistant U.S. attorney who was brought in to prosecute the case, the Dallas real-estate deal was nothing but a variation of the age-old "pyramid" scheme. "At the bottom were about 400 borrowers," he explained, "recruited by the developers and people associated with them and put into little corporations to obtain loans from the bank." Some were encouraged to falsify documents in order to obtain loans, presumably to buy into the sprawling condominium development.

The lure was the time-tested one: how to get something for nothing. The prospectus promised "a return in the neighborhood of $200,000 in the two-year period with no cash output on your part." The victims lured into the scam were by no means what you would call an unsophisticated lot. Among them were lawyers, doctors, politicians, a judge, and even a former member of the Dallas Cowboys.

The initial participants did not contribute any money to the plan. Instead, they were conned into lending their names to be used to enable the promoters to borrow some $500 million in questionable loans at the now-defunct Empire Savings & Loan Bank in Mesquite, Texas. Although this institution was later described as nothing more than "a small brick blob in the parking lot of a strip shopping center outside Dallas," their paperwork was sufficient to convince the FSLIC, the federal guarantor, to pay out $300 million on insured deposits. Empire's assets escalated as the bank used a fairly conventional and normally acceptable procedure that entailed buying brokered deposits and selling off the mortgages.

After the fraud was uncovered by investigative reporters at the *Dallas Morning News,* 25 of the early participants were either indicted or agreed to plead guilty to fraud charges. These were people who had invested little or no money but had received $20,000 or more for their part in the operations and had thus— in some cases unwittingly—furthered the fraud. Yet the promoters seemingly remained out of reach of the law.

The plan worked this way: Back in 1982, several real-estate developers bought a parcel of cheap land that was worth less than $50,000. By selling it back and forth to each other or to their confederates, they inflated the selling price to almost $400,000 in a matter of days. The next step was to start building condominiums on the property, in order to attract several hundred investors and balloon the supposed value of the real estate even further.

Although many of the 25 participants who were indicted claimed ignorance about the true nature of the promoter's scheme, they could not deny the fact that *greed* had been their undoing. Promised at least $20,000 just for their signatures and statements of "net worth," they did not hesitate to stretch the truth, sometimes to the breaking point, in order to cash in on such a surefire investment. One participant signed papers indicating that he held more than $1 million in securities when, in fact, he owned none. Another claimed to be the owner of two homes, which turned out to be nonexistent. A third forged tax returns showing a high income for the previous two years when, in fact, his income was so low that he had not even filed tax returns for those two years.

Not only did many of those indicted find themselves subject to sentences and fines, but they put themselves into debt for bank loans that in some cases totaled hundreds of thousands of dollars, which they could never hope to repay in a lifetime— and all because they were lured into trying to get something for nothing.

On Shaky Ground

Federal investigators say that recently they have uncovered a pattern of similar frauds. Many of these are directed against the Department of Housing and Urban Development in that they involve documents that are deliberately falsified in order to obtain government-backed mortgages. In recent years, more than a dozen real-estate agents and mortgage industry officials have been indicted or convicted in southern New Jersey alone because of their involvement in such schemes. Similar swindles have been reported in Milwaukee, Houston, and Seattle, with total losses of tens of millions of dollars to the government and no one yet knows how many millions more to unwary individual investors who have gotten caught up in the net.

There is great concern that the pattern of such frauds shows all the earmarks of a nationwide operation that moves from region to region applying the same techniques. One of the largest of these frauds has been occurring in the nation's capital, right under the noses of some of the government officials who have been the most embarrassed by the disclosures. Under suspicion have been nearly 500 mortgages that were guaranteed by the Federal Housing Authority in low-income areas of Washington, with a possible loss of $25 million.

"We're very alarmed because there seems to be some sort of whispering campaign among these people [the promoters who were indicted]," says Robert E. Nipp, a spokesman for the government housing agency. "These schemes go from city to city, and it looks as if they use the same routine."

As in the Dallas swindle, the real-estate promoters employ the stratagem of using fraudulent papers to sign up buyers in order to negotiate huge loans through small banks which then receive federal funds to guarantee the loans. Investigators invariably discover, too, that the claimed values of the land, buildings, or other real estate are inflated out of all proportion to their possible worth. Investors are duped into joining the scheme because they see what looks like a risk-free plan to make a lot of money with a ridiculously small down payment, if any at all. What they do not realize is that their signature on mortgages or other legal documents immediately makes them personally liable for the loans secured. Lulled into blissful gratification by the receipt of checks for several thousand dollars for their cooperation, they overlook the real truth. While the swindlers are enjoying the millions of dollars of accumulated loans coming in, the suckers are holding the bag for those very same loans when they go—as they invariably must—into default.

An interesting sidelight is that, in some cases, the government ends up holding the bag for a falsified mortgage. Some imaginative real-estate swindlers have taken out mortgages in the names of prison inmates, newborn babies, and even dead people with cemetery addresses.

"It becomes apparent with each passing indictment that fraud is more extensive than this Court ever thought," said Federal District Judge Stanley Brotman as he sentenced one group of indicted swindlers early in 1986. "The Court cannot close its eyes to the fact that every taxpayer is hurt. Money is being stolen."

The Spectrum of Scams

Among the most widespread real-estate frauds is the multiple sale of landsites, often on property that is totally unsuited for residential use and that could never be developed for private homes. Typical was the case some years ago of a development called Lake Havasu Estates, whose name was deliberately selected to confuse prospective buyers with Lake Havasu City, a successful resort area 40 miles away. Carved out of the desert near the Colorado River, the legitimate Havasu became a city of 10,000 people, noted as the site of the famed London Bridge, which had been bought from England and rebuilt in western Arizona with considerable publicity.

Lake Havasu Estates, however, consisted of thousands of acres of barren land with nothing in evidence but a portable sales office and a few bumpy streets. The cactus-covered land had no accessible water supply, sewage disposal, or utilities. But high-pressure salesmen were selling lots, sight unseen, from coast to coast.

"We were led to believe," said one disenchanted land investor later, "that this was the same property that had been developed by the multimillion-dollar McCulloch Corporation at the London Bridge site and that it was an ongoing operation that was attracting a lot of satisfied buyers." Only after making a sizable investment and reading an ad for the real Havasu development did he realize his unfortunate mistake. Despite persistent attempts to recoup his down payment, including the hiring of an attorney to represent him, he ended up with nothing but a useless acre and a half of wasteland.

To compound the insult, many purchasers of questionable real estate have discovered that the very same parcel of land they bought had been resold three or four times over. On one occasion it was testified at federal hearings that a developer had resold each of his lots as many as eight times to different buyers.

"It was unnerving enough to know that my lot was deeded to seven other people," said one of the victims who testified, "but to think that we had been suckered into laying down money for a pile of earth you wouldn't want to assign to the town dump—that was the real kick in the guts!"

Another shady practice is to sell land on what is known as a "contract for deed." American consumers are accustomed to making purchases on the installment plan, so they think nothing of buying land the same way. One of the major persuasions expressed by the real-estate developer is that you can aspire to a much larger land investment if you make a down payment now, followed by periodic installments later. The questionable land developer, however, promotes the "contract for deed" *without making it clear to purchasers that the title to the land is acquired only after the final payment has been made. A buyer can make installments for years without ever obtaining an actual recorded title. If the promoter goes bankrupt or simply disappears, the purchaser loses his entire investment.* In many cases, purchasers are never provided with a clear title to the land, even after they have completed payments and discharged all their financial obligations. This little oversight, often deliberate, has swindled thousands of buyers out of real estate that legally should be theirs.

Another misleading tactic on the part of spurious developers is to sell land *shares* rather than individual plots or homesites. In a typical deal of this nature, one purchaser discovered after making investments totaling several thousand dollars that he did not hold title to any specific lot at all but rather owned *one two-thousandth* of an interest in 450 undivided acres of land, much of which was unsuitable for building sites. In essence, he and 1,999 other such owners would have had to fight each other for possession of the few lots that were minimally adaptable. As it turned out, the developer had already absconded with the money, and the bank holding the worthless mortgage repossessed the land and was trying to sell it off to an industrial client at a huge discount.

Not a few swindlers have used investors' funds to make down payments on land, mortgaged the whole development, and then resold the land to other unsuspecting investors. By the time the bank has foreclosed on their mortgage, the dishonest developers have long since pulled up stakes and vanished, leaving innocent purchasers to fret and fume.

Another kind of scam is the so-called "timber investment." It preys on prospective victims who not only see a way to make substantial profits but who are concerned about the environment and the preservation of our forests. As the promoters tell prospects so glibly, forest investment is like purchasing gold because there are only so many woodlands in the U.S. and tree farming is big business. "We sell you forest land when the trees are small and relatively worthless," said one pitchman, "and then when the trees grow to commercial size in 10 years or so, your investment is worth 20 times what it was when you bought in." The only flaw in his argument was that the forest tract he was selling consisted mainly of swampland where there were almost no commercial stands of trees and where loggers would have needed amphibious machines just to get to the location.

In Ruston, Louisiana, a "timber deal" promoted by a local group sounded so attractive that the developers' friends and even relatives invested money in it. It turned out to be a "Ponzi" operation. People who invested early received interest checks every 60 days at the high rate of 30 percent annually—until the bubble burst and the checks stopped coming. By the time the

promoters filed for bankruptcy, they had taken in an estimated $8 to $10 million yet had assets of barely half a million dollars. Among the losers were bankers, businessmen, a state representative, and the president of a college. One early investor who had seen his money double from some $45,000 to $92,000 was so elated that he put the entire amount right back into the scheme. Now, however, he was at the low end of the chain— in with the investors who were paying for the ones at the top. He lost it all in a matter of weeks.

There is almost no limit to the amount of money that can be lost to real-estate swindles. One of the biggest in history was a $2 billion land-fraud scheme perpetrated largely by two men, Bernard Whitney, a lawyer from California, and Hendricus Kamer, a Dutch real-estate promoter. The men cheated as many as 6,000 investors out of this huge sum through land deals offered as purported tax shelters in Utah, Texas, New York, and California. None of the money allegedly received by the defendants was ever recovered and, under applicable federal laws, the defendants could not be fined or ordered to make restitution to defrauded investors!

Kamer was deported to the Netherlands to face light charges there and Whitney was sentenced to spend six months in a community care facility. The judge explained the lenient sentence by citing that Whitney, then 66, was in poor health and might not survive a jail term. The biggest mystery of all, however, was what happened to the money acquired from the sale of what turned out to be hugely overpriced desert lots. Whitney claimed that he was unable to make any kind of restitution and his attorney described him as "destitute."

Such are the wages of crime.

Before You Invest In Real Estate . . .

Consider these tips from experienced professionals, whether you are purchasing raw land, homesites, buildings, or any other kind of real estate.

- See the property in person or, at the very least, have it inspected by someone you can trust who is capable of evaluating it.

- If purchasing from a salesperson, ask for a copy of the federal property report required by law of most large developers. Take this home and study it carefully before reaching any decision, since it contains vital details about such matters as the nature of the property, rights and titles, waivers, restrictions, and the "cooling off" period during which you have the option of changing your mind and canceling the agreement.

- Show your attorney the sales contract *before* you sign anything. He is better qualified than you are to look at the small print and interpret legal terminology.

- Check the background and credentials of the firm(s) making the offering.

- Never expect that you will get something for nothing or a lot for a little.

- Make sure that funds turned over for investment are placed in a secure escrow account at a bank and are not readily accessible to any individuals.

- Before buying, check with your state Real Estate Department, Attorney General's office, Securities Division, and/or your local Better Business Bureau.

ALERT!

Chapter 7

PAINFUL DRILLING

ALERT!

It was well known in the early 1970s that more than three dozen high-ranking executives at General Electric, including the board chairman, had invested in the oil and gas drilling programs of a company called Home-Stake Production. So had top people in the First National City Bank, the United States Trust Company, Procter & Gamble, Western Union, and a number of prestigious Wall Street firms. The drilling programs offered in an energy-conscious America were also attractive to a wealth of show-business people, including Jack Benny, Andy Williams, Candice Bergen, Walter Matthau, and Liza Minnelli.

The Tulsa-based Home-Stake, with interests in a Venezuelan oil venture and drilling leases in central California, was no ordinary oil company. It wooed investors with promises of 400 percent returns on their investments as well as huge tax savings on deductible energy operations. Home-Stake was also what was later described as "the most spectacular swindle in U.S. history, a scheme aimed exclusively at rich and financially astute people."

The man behind the Home-Stake fraud, Robert S. Trippet, had to be a genius to entice such an imposing list of victims. After all, as *Time* magazine later reported, "Getting penny pincher Jack Benny to kick $300,000 into a shaky oil scheme is no easy job." Moreover, Trippet was able to extend his manipulative skills over a period of some 18 years, milking all the major outposts of wealth from New York and Palm Beach to Los Angeles and Palm Springs before his fraudulent empire began to collapse.

The perpetrator of one of the greatest flimflams in the history of the American oil industry—which has had its share of phony deals and rigged leases—was completely unlike the typical promoter of such ventures. A well-educated lawyer and conservative dresser, Trippet was equally at home in the boardrooms of giant corporations, the offices of Wall Street financiers, and the colorful environment of Hollywood. Perhaps that is one reason he was so successful at convincing the rich and famous that he was of their breed and interested in showing them how to share the wealth.

Summing up this classic oil and gas swindle, one publisher reminded readers that the story "reveals the surprisingly inept ways in which many wealthy people manage their money" and concluded that "the Home-Stake affair is a startling reminder of the dangers lurking in every financial opportunity."

The Slippery Strategem Of T. Scales

You do not have to be a corporate officer or large investor to get hooked by one of the many oil and gas scams that have plagued the energy industry almost from the time petroleum was first discovered in America in commercial quantities. The ease with which the average investor can get hooked was described by the Alabama Securities Commission when it cited the case of a company called Resources, Ltd., operated by one T. Carlyle Scales, a resident of Atlanta who also maintained a home in the resort area of Gulf Shores, on the Gulf of Mexico.

Scales attracted the attention of several doctors who lived in the area with tales of oil wells in Texas that were producing well and would be big money earners. Best of all, he explained, they could get in on his heady share-the-wealth program by investing $50,000 each for a limited partnership in Resources, Ltd. Under his program, Scales explained, "without going into all the technical details," each investment would double itself within two or three years—perhaps within one year. Another big advantage to the deal, he said, was that investors would be able to claim a huge tax write-off because of the nature of the energy business.

Scales also contacted other investors in the Mobile, Alabama, area and lured them into the deal with similar promises of a fast buck. None of these investors was given a prospectus, financial statement, offering circular, or other disclosure information. The startling truth is that they were not even provided with documented evidence of their participation after they had made their $50,000 investment.

Three investors, eager to join the parade, were unable to come up with the cash. Instead, they were conned into issuing letters of credit to Scales which he could take to a bank as collateral for loans. No need to worry, Scales assured them. The profit from the wells would be more than enough to pay off the letters of credit.

Three other investors, ultimately dismayed by the lack of progress of the venture, demanded the return of their investment. Scales complied by giving them promissory notes for the amount of their contribution—notes which matured but were never paid.

Scales managed to keep investors on the hook and out of his hair by periodically mailing newsletters with glowing reports about the drilling program and the potential of the wells in Texas. Great things were expected. When his communications campaign began to falter and some of the investors became suspicious, he announced a big new deal. He, too, he admitted, was becoming annoyed at the sluggishness of the operations in Texas. So he was withdrawing the interests of Resources, Ltd., in these oil fields and transferring them to natural gas wells in Kentucky.

While damning the Texas operation to his investors, behind their backs he was touting its potential to the Merchants Bank in Foley, Alabama, in order to secure a $400,000 loan.

The sad ending to this story is that 17 Alabama investors were ripped off for some $1.8 million and 36 out-of-state investors for more than $4.5 million by the time the fraud was uncovered. They had all been led to believe that Resources, Ltd., actually owned the wells that were being drilled when, in actuality, the partnership held rights to only a very small percentage of each well. No matter how successful the production might ever have become, the investors stood little chance of breaking even, let alone making any money out of the deal.

Behind the Resources, Ltd., scam was an old familiar tactic used in so many oil and gas frauds: inventing false or misleading information to lure investors and keep them on the hook while the promoters of the scheme made use of their money in less-than-ethical ways. Even when the Securities and Exchange Commission or other government agencies take action against these questionable operators, they often are unable to do more than give the hustlers a slap on the wrist and warn off additional would-be investors.

Such was the case when the Securities and Exchange Commission filed charges in federal court in Washington, D.C., against Major Explorations, Inc., a small Texas-based oil and gas firm, asserting that the company illegally pumped up the price of its stock by distributing false claims about its petroleum reserves and drilling success. The company officers named in the alleged securities fraud were able to settle the SEC suit, without admitting or denying the charges, by paying back a modest amount of money and relinquishing some of their shares of stock. As for the investors left holding stock that had once been inflated to more than twice its initial price, they were likely to end up taking a bath when the price of the stock eventually dropped.

More Cons and Conjurers

A flimflam artist operating on a somewhat grander scale was Christos Netelkos, who successfully exploited the blind enthusiasm of investors for oil technology stocks in the early 1980s and ultimately bilked them out of hundreds of thousands of dollars. He used a classic approach: establishing a penny-stock company called Falcon Sciences, inflating its zero worth to about three dollars a share, and touting capabilities it did not possess. Falcon was promoted through ruthless salesmanship as a high-tech company in the field of enhanced oil-recovery technology (methods for increasing the amount of crude oil recovery from old or marginally productive wells).

"Many of the several thousand victims were small investors," reported *Financial World* in the spring of 1985, "but what's even more tragic is that the SEC usually does not catch up with stock manipulation until after it has happened."

According to court papers, the company issued almost seven million shares of "clearly unauthorized and probably counterfeit" common stock. The sale of some three million of these shares to the general public brought a profit of $3.4 million, which was then widely publicized to stockholders as "oil and gas revenues." What the shareholders did not learn was that most of the money had already been diverted to a Swiss bank account controlled by Netelkos.

It would have upset them even more had they known that Netelkos, a onetime hairdresser and an "inveterate wheeler-dealer," had served 3 years of an 11-year sentence after conviction for a long record of securities violations. When his past caught up with him, Netelkos conveniently disappeared and became a fugitive, but not before he had made a bundle on another bogus company supposedly formed for the secondary recovery of petroleum, Reliance Oil & Gas.

Several victims had sunk huge amounts into Falcon. One big loser, ironically, was the chief of a county criminal identification bureau who had more than $200,000 tied up in virtually worthless stock. Never once did he suspect that Netelkos, then masquerading under the name Christopher J. Nickos, was the same man who was to be pictured on a U.S. Department of Justice poster headlined WANTED BY U.S. MARSHALS and offering a reward for information leading to his arrest. This unfortunate victim could ill afford the loss, since he had withdrawn all his savings, mortgaged his home, and borrowed from his mother in order to invest in the shell game manipulation.

There is no season for these flimflam artists, who seem able to dupe investors no matter what the real state of the economy by creating their own "market" conditions. When oil prices are high and energy companies are booming, for example, the boiler-room operator gets on the phone and gives the following kind of pitch: "Mr. Smith, I'm calling you specially because I know you are the kind of investor who wants to take advantage of the ballooning demand for oil and gas. The XYZ Petroleum Company is an aggressive, no-nonsense producer in one of the biggest oil patches in the U.S.A. and...."

What happens when petroleum prices plunge and the bottom falls out of the energy market? The con man simply reverses his pitch: "I'm sure that a man as perceptive as you, Mr. Smith, realizes that the time has never been better for investing in oil and gas leases. With low prices encouraging drivers to consume more gasoline and with oil companies cutting back on exploration and production, you and I know exactly what will happen. We'll be right back where we were a few years ago, with a big shortage on our hands and prices skyrocketing again. But the XYZ Petroleum Company isn't waiting for the crisis to happen. It's out there right now, in one of the biggest fields in Oklahoma, pumping out barrels of cheap oil to sell later at premium prices. . . ."

Officials in the oil-producing states warn that oil and gas scams remain alive and well even during downturns in the industry. During 1985 and 1986, for example, when petroleum prices were weak and the industry was cutting back, there were 850 ongoing investigations of unlawful oil and gas investment activity in five states with significant drilling activity. In Illinois alone, it was reported that more than 1,200 eager investors had been defrauded to the tune of about $14 million during this period. In 1985, the Alabama Securities Commission and the FBI obtained a grand jury indictment against a promoter who had swindled 50 investors out of $6 million through gross misrepresentation of a drilling venture, his experience, and the prospects for success. He was also charged with converting $1 million of investor funds to his own use.

Four Scams and a Schemer

The experienced con man can rationalize almost anything at any time. According to Craig Stancliff, of the Kansas Securities Commission, there are four basic kinds of oil and gas frauds.

1. The sale of fractional interests in a drilling venture which, right from the beginning, is nothing but a dry hole. The promoters lease a plot of undesirable land, rent some false-front drilling equipment that looks good in color photographs, and simply pocket the proceeds. Up until the time they flee with the funds, it is almost impossible to prosecute the officers of this kind of bogus company, because

they can cite thousands of examples of reputable companies that have drilled speculatively and ended up with dry holes.

2. The prediction of a huge "discovery" in a region where there are no known petroleum deposits and where investors can supposedly get in on the ground floor of a really big venture. One such scam selected a remote section of Iowa where there have been no wells and touted the area as having a field "larger than Saudi Arabia." The prospective "pigeons" selected as investors were obviously people who were too far removed from the region to investigate the claims easily.

ALERT!

3. Assistance in making a killing through participation in oil and gas lotteries. Such lotteries are legitimate oil and gas leasing systems making parcels of federal land available to the public, run periodically by the United States Bureau of Land Management. Any U.S. citizen can file for a chance to win a mineral rights lease on any parcel by paying a small entry fee. What inexperienced investors do not realize is that the vast majority of leases have little or no market value and that there may be hundreds of applications for each lease. The system invites fraud on the part of so-called "consultants" who charge exorbitant fees to help would-be participants obtain leases. The con artists use high-pressure tactics, claim inside information, claim to have expert geologists on their staffs who can provide advisory services, and often soak the victim for five times the government's fee for filing.

4. The offering of noncompetitive bids in Alaska, exploiting the popular belief that most of the state is sitting on top of enormous fields of petroleum. Promoters buy leases "over the counter" from the U.S. government or the state of Alaska, then divide them into smaller parcels to sell to the public at exorbitant prices. The areas available to the promoters are ones with no known deposits of oil or gas. When victims protest, after months or even years have

gone by with no drilling activity, that they are concerned about their investment, the promoters capitalize on this dissatisfaction by claiming that they have a waiting list of other participants and offering to sell the investor's rights and recoup his money. There is, of course, a stiff charge for this additional service.

Oil and gas frauds often succeed because of the complexities inherent in the energy industry and the extreme difficulties of proving in court that an operator was really dishonest and not simply the victim of mismanagement or incompetence. A typical case—though one on a much grander scale than any case that had ever been tried before—was that of Robert Sutton, who was cited on the 1982 *Forbes 400* list of prominent executives as an "oil salesman extraordinary," with a net worth of $150 million.

During the 1970s, when OPEC pumped up oil prices fivefold, the U.S. Congress tried to steady America's oil economy by taking several important steps. One was to permit the price of newly discovered oil in the United States produced from "stripper" wells to be tagged at as much as six times that of "old" oil found before 1973.

"The hustlers, big and little, soon caught on," reported an editorial in *Forbes* magazine in the fall of 1984, "and by 1980 as much as 10 percent of U.S. domestic oil was being falsely certified, costing consumers $10 billion. Half of that windfall, investigators claimed, probably went into the pockets of operators like Robert Sutton. From a dead start in 1976, his BPM, Ltd., and other smaller companies bought at least 156 million barrels of old oil, selling it as new or higher-priced stripper oil. Estimates of Sutton's profits ran from $250 million to $500 million."

Although prosecutors brought Sutton to court in the largest criminal case, in dollar terms, ever filed against one man, he was eventually found guilty only of "obstruction of justice" and slapped with a mere three-year prison term.

There have been numerous examples of victims being duped into investing in oil and gas companies that were either operating illegally or openly flouting the law, as in the cases of the operators who turned cheap old oil into expensive new oil, not by chemistry but by fraud. But the real significance of the Sutton case as far as investors are concerned is that many of them can be duped unwittingly into becoming parties to a crime if they are lured by offers of quick riches and fail to investigate the true nature of their participation. Not a few astonished investors in fraudulent businesses (in other fields as well as oil and gas) have found themselves involved in lawsuits, criminal indictments, and court actions as a result of their failure to investigate before investing.

In general, the law takes the position that investors are "participants" and are thus liable to the extent that they were seeking personal profit. If only the investors suffer, that is cause for leniency. If, however—as in the case of the Sutton type of operation—the fraud results in huge losses to innocent consumers, the crime is anything but "victimless" and the courts take a much tougher stance.

The unwary investor can get burned, not once but twice over.

Before You Invest In Oil or Gas . . .

There are many warning signals to look for when it comes to investing in oil and gas ventures, particularly those that are promoted to you by mail or over the phone. Exorbitant claims are the real giveaways. So shy away from any kind of deal when you hear any of the following claims.

- Production is *guaranteed.* If the well does not produce, you get your money back.

- The potential is enormous, but the risks are minimal.

- The firm has inside information and hot tips about the lease or oil field.

- The firm's own executives have invested heavily in the venture.

- The field is one in which new discoveries are just now being made.

- One of the big oil companies is investing money, time, and the efforts of geologists in the area.

- You have been selected as one of only a handful of potential investors solicited.

- You must act *now* if you want to get in on the deal. **ALERT!**

- The program does not have to be registered under federal or state laws because it is a "private placement."

- Another warning flag: The firm's office is in one state, the petroleum operations are in another, and the offerings are in states other than either of these two, thus making investigation more difficult for prospective investors and state securities regulators.

Oil and gas investments are generally complex and take many forms, including limited partnerships, general partnerships, and ownership of fractional undivided interests in leases. Even at best, the most valid drilling partnerships have always been a gamble, simply because of the speculative nature of the petroleum industry and the risks involved. Historically, one of every three such ventures fails to return as much as the original investment, the second may barely break even, and the third will return a profit, though seldom very large.

With the odds against you under the most favorable of circumstances, who needs to fall into the clutches of a swindler?

Chapter 8

PENNY STOCKS— ARE THEY WORTH IT?

James McLelland Smith can tell you everything you ever wanted to know about penny stocks, with plenty of information left over. As chief of the Bureau of Securities of the State of New Jersey in Newark, he has witnessed first-hand a never-ending succession of cases involving penny stocks and the fraudulent practices associated with many of them.

This is one investment field in which a prospective investor should be extremely wary. Certainly, there are a few who get in on the ground floor of a legitimate company and who are fortunate enough to be able to sell out after the stock's price rises. But their profits are most often the result of pure luck. Smith would much rather talk about the size and nature of the trap that lies in wait for the unwary investors whose judgment is dazzled by their belief that they can enter the world of investment through the bargain basement.

Peddling the Pennies

Penny stocks are inherently risky. Typically, the issuer is a small, poorly financed company whose future prospects are extremely uncertain. Because of their low cost and the relatively small number of stockholders, penny stocks are all too often the subject of price manipulation by the firms that take them public and by other broker-dealers who subsequently make a market in the stock.

There are two basic factors involved in any consideration of penny stocks, which actually can range in price anywhere from one cent to about five dollars. First, the issue is often fraudulent to begin with, the only objective being to lure investors into buying a lot of worthless paper. Fraudulent penny stocks can sometimes be distinguished from legitimate low-priced stocks by a careful reading of the prospectus (see page 102). Second, a broker-dealer is needed to promote the issue, his "contribution" to the action being that he has the network and the contacts.

"The key to it all," says Smith, "is the salesperson who usually has no qualifications in the investment field. Many penny-stock salespeople already have minor convictions for hustling or other clashes with the law. Brokers bring them into the action and offer them their 'big chance,' knowing full well that they will not mind stretching a few scruples in order to make a killing." Some of these salespeople, who have no training in securities, are clever enough and persistent enough to earn more than $1 million a year peddling the "pennies."

Penny stocks are seldom sold initially by prospectus but rather by phone. The salespeople, despite their nonprofessional background, are usually well trained in the nuances of telephone solicitation. They start off in a low-key manner with a pitch that may go something like this: "Mr. Smith, I'd like to introduce myself. I'm a stockbroker and we are making a little survey to find out what people in your neighborhood are interested in knowing about promising investments."

After they line up prospects who do not discourage them outright or hang up, they place a second call. Now their voice is edged with excitement. They have just received inside information on a new stock issue that holds great promise, especially for people who might only want to make a small investment. The "double-your-money" pitch might be used if the prospect's ears seem to prick up. The chances are that the salesperson will do no more than paint a rosy picture and promise to keep the prospect posted. The idea, of course, is to let him dream a little so that he will be an easier mark for a bigger sale.

The third phone call is likely to start off with a phrase like this: "I've just been talking with the president of the XYZ Company and he says. . . ." Another ploy is to say, "I'm holding 3,000 shares in your name. I had hoped to reserve 5,000, but there has been such a big demand. . . ." Now the hot advice is to *buy*—and at once! The prospect is urged to withdraw his money from the bank and send it right in to the company. The prospectus for the stock? Oh, that will be sent by return mail, with a detailed description of this company that is on the verge of a big financial breakthrough.

After the customer has sent in his money and then received the prospectus, he is likely to be shocked. He finds out, too late, that the company has very little capital, that the principals are inexperienced, and that, indeed, in some instances, it has not yet been decided quite what kind of a business venture is going to be undertaken.

Here are some actual excerpts from the prospectuses issued on three companies in 1986.

- "These securities offer a high degree of risk and the company is and will be significantly underfinanced. It is highly probable the proceeds from this offering will be insufficient for any sustained, ongoing operation and there is a substantial likelihood that the company will be unsuccessful. . . ."

- "The purchase hereof should be considered only by persons who can afford the loss of their entire investment."

- "The company is currently significantly dependent upon the personal efforts and abilities of its 2 officers, neither of whom has had any relevant experience in (a) assessing business(es) to determine whether such business(es) would provide good business opportunities for the Company or (b) locating and/or acquiring existing business(es) and/or acquiring assets to establish subsidiary business(es) and neither of whom will be devoting significant time to the Company's proposed day-to-day business activities."

The last-quoted prospectus also stated, flat out, that one of the two officers had been "enjoined, suspended and subject to various disciplinary proceedings in the securities business...."

In talking about the speculative nature of investing in its stock, one prospectus stated, "The main risk factors include the fact that the Company has no operating history, that it must rely upon inexperienced management, that it has no specific business or use of proceeds, and that it is a blind-pool offering."

"Blind pool" is a term used with some of these penny-stock offerings to indicate that the investors and the promoter do not know exactly where or how the money invested will be put to work, if at all. Reporting that securities administrators were worried about the proliferation of blind pools, the *New York Times* explained in an editorial in early 1986, "The offerings are designed to raise a bankroll. How that bankroll may be used by the deal's manager is often described only in the broadest terms. For example, while some blind-pool prospectuses will outline an area of investment, such as stocks, real estate, or television stations—even the acquisition of companies—other prospectuses promise only that the manager will seek profitable opportunities."

What Lies Behind the Lure

How can you lose much on a stock that sells for only five or ten cents a share? Sure, it may be a gamble, but isn't it worth a flyer when penny stocks have been known to boom from a few cents to four or five dollars?

Just as people become hooked on the idea of betting on the horses, buying tickets to lotteries, or playing the slot machines at a casino, so they become intrigued with investing in a colorful array of ingenious devices and imaginative services that are largely predestined for failure but that stand a thousand-in-one chance of breaking into the big money. For several years, it was considered a pleasant pastime to own stocks in companies that were marketing reuseable toothpicks, onion-odor remover, asparagus cutters, or vitaminized snuff.

Sadly, the con artists saw that there was a gold mine in penny stocks, which could be sold by the hundreds of thousands

to substantial investors and which lent themselves perfectly to high-pressure tactics. They were ideal come-ons for boiler-room operations, which consist of banks of telephones manned by glib salespeople who have no scruples about making the most outrageous claims. Moreover, the fast-talking promoters could promise almost anything with little fear that the stocks they touted could be investigated quickly or easily.

Is the business really that big or important? In Colorado, when the Denver penny-stock market collapsed in 1982 largely as a result of fraudulently inflated prices, hundreds of millions of dollars were lost by thousands of unfortunate investors. Following the collapse, new waves of buying and selling simply set the stage all over again for another generation of fraud. One study revealed that 45 percent of the penny stocks surveyed were being sold by promoters who were convicted felons, securities violators, reputed crime figures, or who were under investigation for financial misdealing.

Stocks with no value at all but selling for 10 cents a share were being promoted by con artists who could use any of a variety of manipulative techniques to make sales, eventually kiting the price to three or four dollars. Those on the inside could take their money and flee. The rest of the purchasers were left with fistfuls of worthless paper.

What it boils down to is that often the only people who end up winners in the penny-stock game are the brokers, the insiders, and the company principals who devised the scheme to begin with. What the customers frequently end up with are a bunch of "dog" stocks that no one wants to buy because the companies they represent have very little past and no future.

Among the promoters of the "dogs" have been: a brokerage firm in Jersey City that was banned from offering new securities after a federal judge found the firm engaged in a stock manipulation scheme for a company that manufactured an ointment alleged to grow hair on bald men, a California company that raised $3 million even though its prospectus said that the company had no plan of operation and did not know what business it would be in, and a company called Dentec that raised about $1 million on the penny-stock market even while candidly admitting that it would probably be illegal—as it eventually turned out to be—for it to obtain the state dental license it needed to begin business.

A Losing Proposition

The dice are often loaded heavily against purchasers of penny stocks, not only because of ultimate business failures by the companies involved but because the officers and insiders purchase stock at a fraction of what the public pays. A typical example is that of a company called Roltec, which told prospective investors that it was developing a high-tech product called a "squirm drive mechanism." Ten officers, directors, and other insiders purchased 12 million shares of the stock (or 75 percent) for $12,000, in blatant contrast to the 4 million shares purchased by the public for $1 million. In such situations, the promoter-brokers hype the sale of the stock, driving up the

99

price. Typically, the promoters then sell out with a fat profit, the stock price collapses, and investors are the ones left holding the bag.

The situation became so uncontrollable in Utah that the governor formed a Securities Fraud Task Force, which spent about 10 months investigating the nature and extent of the problem in that state. "In recent years," said the resulting report, "Utah has gained a reputation as the site of an inordinate amount of securities fraud and other investment frauds. Ten of these frauds have involved over 9,000 Utahns, who have experienced a loss of approximately $200 million. In addition to direct investment losses, these frauds have caused a loss of confidence in Utah's lawful securities market, made it more difficult for legitimate businesses to raise capital, and fostered a negative image of Utah's people and institutions. The indirect financial losses to Utahns may thus be significantly greater than the direct losses."

The persistence and brazenness of the penny-stock manipulators is such, however, that statewide counterattacks often do no more than cause temporary setbacks or force the perpetrators to move their operations to another locale. Within a year or so of the Utah Task Force report, penny stocks were right back in circulation.

"The Kenneth Brailsford affair may mark a milestone in the unsavory history of penny stocks," reported a June 30, 1986, *Business Week* editorial. Brailsford was charged by the Utah Securities Division with reaping at least $100,000 in illegal profits through stock manipulation. A penny-stock broker, he had reportedly paid associates to purchase virtually all 2.5 million shares of the initial public offering of Freedom Coin Company at a penny a share. Secretly, however, the purchasers then sold their shares to Brailsford, who began selling the stock to the public in small amounts, thereby driving up the price.

As penny-stock investors saw the Freedom Coin Company issue move up, they snapped up shares as quickly as Brailsford fed them into the market. Within two months, the price rose from 7¢ to $1.10. It was then that the Utah regulators halted trading, at which point the price slid back to 20¢.

As decisive as Utah's action was against Brailsford, the first action of its kind in the state, there was still a long way to go.

More than 40 other investigations were being conducted and the regulators admitted that they were not sure just what the penalties would be for those involved in many of the cases because no penalties had ever been imposed before in this type of stock manipulation.

Getting out of a penny-stock deal is no easy matter for investors, especially for the uninitiated. "If the customer starts making noises about getting his money back," says New Jersey Securities Chief James McLelland Smith, "he is made to look a little foolish and is told that the price has already doubled and it would be silly to sell at this stage. He is always put off and told to wait just a week or so. When he phones again, a sweet voice informs him that the salesperson is 'out of town,' 'on vacation,' or otherwise unavailable."

When matters finally come to a head and the shareholder literally demands his money back, he is told, "OK, I'll do what I can for you, but this is a very poor time to sell." It is at this point that he discovers how great a difference there is between the "asked" and "bid" price for the stock—the former being the figure on paper and the latter the amount the broker will actually pay. If the customer ends up with 50 percent of what he paid originally, he is lucky.

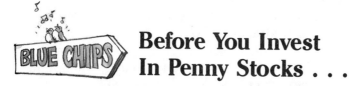

Before You Invest In Penny Stocks . . .

There are, of course, many inexpensive stocks that are legitimate and are used to finance valid entrepreneurial enterprises. The question is, how do you distinguish these stocks from the penny stocks that are merely elaborate schemes to part you and your money?

First of all, beware of high-pressure, unsolicited telephone calls urging you to invest in a real bargain. The fraudulent penny-stock broker has a "boiler room," a bank of telephones manned by high-pressure salespeople who tout stocks with outrageous promises. Beware of claims that the stock will double soon and demands that you make an on-the-spot decision and pay immediately. Suggestions that the broker has inside information or that manipulative techniques are being used to raise the stock's price should be viewed very suspiciously. They are danger signs of the penny-stock game in which many buyers are losers.

Equally important, if you are not immediately turned off and certain that the offering is a fraud, is to obtain a prospectus and read it carefully. The prospectus is a required document that is supposed to contain full disclosure of all facts and risks involved in the offering. No broker or salesperson involved with legitimate stock offerings will try to dissuade you from this step. In the end, what you learn—or do not learn—from the prospectus should be a basic factor in determining whether or not you invest your money. You should regard as a red flag anything you read in the prospectus that contradicts what a salesperson has claimed. The prospectus will include the following sections, among others.

- *Management:* Facts about the principals in the company.

- *Financial health:* Capital, debts, and an accountant's report.

- *Dilution:* Charts or data to show how many shares of stock will be given or already have been transferred to principals or promoters at little or no cost.

ALERT!

- *Proceeds:* The use to which investment money will be put, both to develop the products or services and to pay salaries and taxes.

- *Product:* The degree to which company products or services have been developed, tested, and proven useful.

- *Conflicts of interest:* Interest-free loans to company officials and other internal benefits that aid the promoters but are of no value to investors.

- *Litigation:* Lawsuits filed against the company and other restrictive actions that could hinder development.

Finally, find out whether the stock is registered with your state Securities Division or the federal SEC. Such registration is not an indication of approval or testimony to the soundness of the company, but it does confirm that the facts about the company and the offering have been disclosed.

Chapter 9

PONZIS AND PYRAMIDS

ALERT!

When Kenneth Oxborrow first began to talk about his investment scheme, he had a lot of listeners. What he said made sense to them—and they certainly wanted it to. It was a time, in early 1981, when interest rates were high and crop prices low. So the promises that Oxborrow made to his farm-oriented neighbors and others in the agricultural areas of Washington State were irresistible. He claimed that he could double the money of everyone who invested in his fledgling firm, Wheatland Investments Co. Not only that, but they would be guaranteed earnings of 2½ percent *per week.*

How could this 33-year-old former farmer, with no experience in the world of finance, manage to devise an investment plan that even the most sophisticated financiers had never dreamed of? Quite simple, said Oxborrow. They merely had overlooked a rudimentary method of making profits in commodities that he had stumbled upon because of his knowledge of agriculture and crop production.

As he explained to the first wave of eager investors, he had been dabbling in commodities futures, putting small amounts of money into contracts that would hold for him large quantities of grain, sugar, potatoes, or other produce. Since he bought when the price was low and sold when the price was high, he pocketed the difference, making thousands of dollars on each transaction.

If he could do that as an individual, he explained, why not form a company and let his friends and neighbors in on a good thing? Thus was born a get-rich "Ponzi" scheme.

It was hard not to believe the young man, especially not when those who had known him as a relatively poor farmer saw him purchase a palatial $350,000 beach home at Moses Lake and place an order for the first of two private planes. His plan looked even more convincing when some of the early investors in Wheatland were seen enjoying pleasant changes in lives that had been devoid of luxury. "It was like Christmas," said one local executive later. "You never saw so many Cadillacs driving along roads that had once been the province of rattling potato trucks and dusty pickups."

For some three years, prosperity brightened the lives of many an investor in Washington, California, Montana, Idaho, and Oregon as Oxborrow lived up to his glorious promise and rewarded their confidence with a steady flow of earnings. In all, more than 900 people pumped a total of $58.5 million into the Wheatland Company. Some were wealthy people, like a successful crop duster who contributed $240,000 to the scheme, a corporate attorney whose commitments totaled $160,000, and the members of a newly formed investment group, which invested almost half a million dollars in the venture. But many were people of average means who mortgaged their homes, took out loans on their farms, or dipped into life savings.

By late 1983, with increasing grumbling on the part of hundreds of investors who had failed to enjoy any new luxuries or see any signs of payment checks, a few cracks were starting to appear in the once-formidable structure of Wheatland Investments Co. For one thing, the Securities Division of the state of Washington discovered that Oxborrow was not licensed to trade in commodities. More to the point, subsequent investigations revealed that less than five percent of the $58.5 million invested in the firm had really gone into futures contracts.

Where had all the money gone? Some had been used to gild the lily, as it were, dispensing dramatic profits to a handful of early investors as a means of luring other victims. It was the old Ponzi scheme, the classic formula of inducing waves of investors to pour their money into a plan whose early investors were paid handsome "profits." The very first to profit, of course, was Kenneth Oxborrow, with his lakeside home, private planes, Rolls Royces, luxury vacations, and other amenities. In addition,

Oxborrow had treated his wife to the purchase of a couple of high-fashion clothing stores, built a waterslide park near Moses Lake, and dabbled in other real-estate and financial dealings.

The sad truth of the matter, though, was that a great deal of the $58.5 million had simply been squandered through bad judgment, huge losses in the commodities market, and shaky investments.

The fantasy dissolved in August 1984 when Wheatland was shut down by Washington State regulators and Kenneth Oxborrow filed what was described as "the largest personal bankruptcy ever seen in these parts." In October, he pleaded guilty in both federal and state courts to charges of theft and securities fraud. In January 1985, he entered prison to start serving concurrent 4- and 15-year sentences.

One other factor in this preposterous scheme fits the classic Ponzi mold. Although Oxborrow left behind an embarrassed and sometimes bitter community when he was led off to jail, many of his victims stood firmly behind him, professed faith in his innocence, and even displayed anger at the state's interference at a time when they believed the company might have effected a turnaround and recouped their money. This was particularly true of those in the agricultural center of Moses Lake who had known "Kenny" since high-school days or were close to his wife's family, which had been farming in central Washington for several generations.

Said Theresa Whitmarsh, a journalist who covered the Oxborrow story for the daily paper in Wenatchee, Washington, "Even when Oxborrow's lifestyle raised eyebrows, his generosity and gentlemanliness endeared. Simply put, people liked the young man. For that matter, many still do. With his medium build, medium height, and neatly trimmed medium-brown hair, there was nothing about him—physically—to set him apart from his neighbors. All the easier to believe his good fortune could be theirs."

Charles Ponzi's Plan

It is true of many Ponzi schemes that the principal swindlers attract their prospective victims by radiating an aura of confidence, camaraderie, and the assurance of wanting to share the wealth. In some cases, the promoters even believe that the schemes will work and that they have discovered some kind of magic formula overlooked by professional financiers. Then, when they realize there are hitches but that they could profit enormously by using other peoples' money, they invent a company and make all kinds of exorbitant promises.

Such was the case with Charles Ponzi (from whom the name of the swindle derives). An Italian immigrant who moved to Boston in 1919, he learned that he could make a small profit by buying International Postal Reply Coupons (IPRCs), which were redeemed for stamps in a number of countries. If he were to buy them at a low rate in a weak-currency country like Spain and then redeem them at a higher price in the United States, he could make a profit on the widely varying rates of exchange.

Greed, however, quickly overran his modest intentions and he began to solicit investments from other people on the promise that they could expect a 40 percent return in just three months, at a time when normal interest rates were only 5 percent. The plan might have worked had there been enough IPRCs in circulation to support the large-scale purchases. But the coupons were distributed in very limited quantities, expressly for the convenience of postal customers who used international mails. By the time interest in the scheme had escalated and Ponzi saw orders flooding in, he was totally obsessed with the idea of making huge amounts of money. By giving some of the investors the 40 percent returns promised—using the money of new participants to pay off earlier ones—he baited the trap, and he was not averse to promising new investors 50 percent returns in 90 days, and eventually 100 percent.

Even after Boston newspapers and law officials exposed the nature of the swindle, money continued to pour into Ponzi's office from victims who were still convinced that he had a good thing going and that they, too, could profit from his ingenuity. Many of those who lost heavily later blamed Massachusetts authorities for butting in and "victimizing" Charles Ponzi.

Although the Ponzi caper fleeced uncounted numbers of Bostonians out of a total of $10 million (a staggering sum in those days), the records revealed that this little-educated immigrant from Italy had actually purchased less than $50 worth of International Postal Reply Coupons, most of them at the very start of the operation.

A New Lease on Lies

One of the startling facts about the Ponzi scam is that, although it has been around for more than 65 years in one form or another and is one of the easiest swindles to detect, *it is more prevalent today than ever before.* Even more astonishing is the fact that similar schemes are snaring many investors who have large sums to invest and who are supposedly experienced and sophisticated in the matter of finances.

According to the North American Securities Administrators Association (NASAA), "The driving force behind this renaissance of the Ponzi swindle is the recent explosion of financial services and often bewildering new investments available to the public. In this crowded and fast-changing marketplace, Ponzi promoters have an increasing number of 'costumes' at their disposal with which to dress up their schemes and shield them from ready detection. So it is that the task of spotting the Ponzi scheme has become more difficult than ever."

The facts bear out NASAA's warning that "this con game now appears to be the biggest single fraud threat confronting average American investors." State securities regulators have been quoted as fearing that it is "now reaching epidemic proportions."

In a sense, investors themselves—through their eagerness to leap into a "get-rich-quick" plan—are to blame for the prevalence of such swindles, which function in a financial atmosphere where *massive profits* are touted, even by some of the formerly conservative banking and brokerage houses. A few daring souls have even been known to invest deliberately in what they have spotted as budding Ponzi schemes, convinced that they could anticipate the course of action and, at the right moment, take their money and run. Besides being morally and legally questionable, this kind of Russian roulette is hardly recommended for the sensible investor.

One variation on the Ponzi scheme, in which a few get rich at the expense of the multitudes, involved the case of a 23-

year-old busboy who raised $7.3 million in early 1985 from 2,800 investors in Ohio by promising to double their money in 60 to 90 days. He practiced the simple expedient of soliciting funds to underwrite the mass-scale purchase of rock-concert tickets, which were then to be scalped at premium prices. By paying out "interest" to initial participants and thus "proving" that his claims were justified and his promises reliable, he duped hundreds of others into putting their money into his hands. The scheme collapsed when he reached a phase-out point and was unable to continue paying interest. Though he was later sued for almost $40 million by disgruntled investors who had lost their shirts, the state securities regulators reported that no more than $1 million would ever be recovered.

The range of Ponzi-type offerings is a tribute to the imagination and ingenuity of the promoters of these big swindles. In Utah, for example, the organist at a mortuary came up with the idea of soliciting the bereaved widows who were his boss's clients. By offering them high returns on what turned out to be nonexistent bonds in a fictitious finance company, he bilked his victims out of $16.5 million before he was caught. In Alabama, a con man made a mint in a bogus plan that involved the resale of designer jeans. In Texas, a stylish-looking lady charmed investors out of $17 million by offering them shares in a phony chain of silver-recycling plants. And in Maryland, a promoter collected some $4 million from Baltimore-area residents by promising them huge returns on largely nonexistent investments in diamonds and secondary mortgages. His qualifications? He was the owner of a poultry stand, which suggests that he certainly knew where to go after the prize chickens!

Swindles of this kind can involve just about any kind of a deal you might imagine, from gold mines and synthetic rubies to hydroponic farming, windmills, tropical islands, and adaptations of equipment used in outer space. But the bottom line for prospective investors is always the same: the promise, indeed the *guarantee,* that they will receive returns on their investment far higher than any going rates.

The promoters rely heavily, too, on what has been described as the "herd instinct." The start-up may be slow, with a trickle of investors who take the bait. But once the plan builds up momentum, word of mouth alone is almost enough to speed the operation into high gear. For this reason, swindlers focus their initial efforts with demography in mind. They may aim at people in the entertainment world, for example, knowing that word of a few successful participants will spread rapidly to others in the profession. In recent cases, such momentum was generated by concentrating on a large church congregation, professional football players, and, of all things, an attorney's association.

The same focus is effective when applied regionally, confining the initial activities to, say, an Air Force base, a single New England city, or a wealthy resort community. The early participants unwittingly aid and abet the swindler by passing along sometimes "confidential, inside" information that a financial killing can be made by those in the know.

Often, the initial participants in Ponzi scams are rewarded with handsome returns on their investment, sometimes at interest rates that are astonishingly higher than the promoters originally promised them. Many of these people, however, are so elated with their success that they turn right around and put their money back where it came from, often losing almost everything in the end.

On the Alert For Ponzis

Here are nine basic rules to follow to avoid getting clobbered by the Ponzi operators of the financial netherworld.

---

1. Ignore promises of high, guaranteed profits, the trademark of the Ponzi scam. Legitimate investment plans not only address themselves conservatively to any discussion of profits but rigorously avoid any promise of specific percentages over any given period.

---

2. Avoid any kind of investment that is not described clearly, in detail, and without hedging. Swindlers often declare that the specifics are "too technical" to describe in layman's

language. They may also avoid mentioning names on the grounds that the geniuses behind the plan "wish to remain anonymous."

3.   Check out the promoters' credentials and background carefully through reliable sources that can alert you to any illegal acts or questionable practices that may discolor their records.

4.   Obtain information about the proposed offering from the state Securities Division and/or Better Business Bureau in the locales involved. If you detect or suspect any violations of the law or securities registration, do other investors a favor by reporting your doubts to these organizations or other pertinent agencies.

ALERT!

5.   Demand detailed information *in writing.* Not only are you well within your rights to ask for documentation, but you will have every right to be concerned if the promoter is reluctant or hedges by asserting that such data is "confidential" or "classified."

6.   Verify the claims and promises made by the promoter. Swindlers often try to imply that the offering is registered with a government agency, has the stamp of approval of Dun & Bradstreet, or has been cleared through such-and-such trust company. Victims too often accept such claims at face value and fail to verify the assertions.

7.   Take the stand that "seeing is believing" and ask to visit the promoter's office or tour the plant where the "fabulous new product" is being manufactured. Suspicion will quickly set in if you are told that unfortunately the office is being "renovated" or the plant is "under tight security" and hence is off-limits to everyone except employees.

8.   Back away from plans that offer "deferred" payments, where you have to invest today but will not see any products or evidence of ownership until tomorrow. If, after

113

investing, you are pressured into reinvesting or letting your profits "roll over," investigate at once.

9.   Be on the alert for any kind of unbusinesslike conduct on the part of the promoters, including the inability to reach them through phone calls or by mail. The farther along the route to disaster a Ponzi plan may be, the more impossible it becomes for victims to obtain information or get through to the promoters.

ALERT!

Even with the best of communications, participants in Ponzi schemes are likely to be outtalked, outflanked, and outmaneuvered by the promoters. As one investor in the phony Wheatland Investments Co. scheme said sadly, "They would call me every week and tell me how many thousands of dollars I had made the week before and I'd write the figures down in my notebook. They looked so good on notebook paper. I should have written them down on toilet paper."

Ponzis and Pyramids— A Distinction

Closely related in the minds of many to the Ponzi scheme is the "pyramid scheme." Sometimes the two go hand in hand. Yet there is a distinction. The classic Ponzi amounts to little more than robbing an army of Peters to pay a handful of Pauls. As the number of initial investors (the Pauls) grows and the supply of new investors (the Peters) dwindles, the Ponzi bubble bursts under the pressure of meeting the promised interest payments. While some initial payments are actually made in order to drum up new recruits, the vast majority of investors in a Ponzi scheme end up losing all or most of their money.

By comparison, the *pyramid* scheme in its purest form is characterized by a plan in which people invest in the right to sell the investment. Participants make money by selling to new investors, down the pyramid, the right to sell the program to those ever lower in the chain.

Many pyramids attempt to establish their legitimacy by purporting to sell a product. What distinguishes these schemes from legitimate multilevel marketing businesses, according to the Council of Better Business Bureaus, is that the pyramid concentrates mainly on the quick profits to be earned by recruiting others to invest who, in turn, will recruit others, and so on. The merchandise or service to be sold is largely ignored.

The pyramid scheme, which functions much like a chain letter, inevitably collapses as participants attempt to recover their initial, often quite large investment by recruiting new investors from the ever-decreasing number of prospects in a given area.

Sometimes it seems that the more esoteric the scheme, the easier it is to dupe the public. This is true of many pyramid swindles. In Kansas in the spring of 1985, the state securities commission issued a restraining order against a syndicate it accused of operating an illegal scheme that had already taken in $10 million from investors in more than 30 states. The product that was so effectively promoted to eager investors: "Activator Kits," which were to be used to grow fungus cultures that would be sold to an affiliated cosmetics manufacturer at a heady profit. What the 12,000 people who rushed to plunk down their money had failed to find out was that there was no known market for the fungus cultures and that they had not been cleared by the federal government as safe for marketing. Furthermore, the much-publicized cosmetics manufacturing plant was never in commercial operation and there were no product sales of any kind in progress.

The Kansas Securities Commission indicted the promoters when it discovered evidence of the classic pyramid swindle: The syndicate was simply paying off the initial participants, including its own members, "by recruiting an ever-increasing number of investors."

In early 1987, "airplane" pyramids began raking in a lot of money for their promoters. The airplane game is much like a high-stakes version of a chain letter. For an initial payment of $1,000 to $3,000, a participant becomes one of eight so-called "passengers" on a plane. Also on the imaginary plane are four flight attendants and two copilots, who pay nothing. After the pilot (in this case the promoter of the swindle) collects the money from the passengers, each copilot then becomes a pilot, forming two new "airplanes" and taking half the passengers from the old group. Each passenger is then expected to recruit at least one new investor, motivated by the expectation of moving up the line, becoming a pilot, and then collecting a large sum.

A few people besides the promoters can make money if they get into the game early enough—just as they would in the old chain-letter routine. But all the other would-be pilots lose their money with no chance of collecting. The procedure has been described as a "scam which requires a rapid flare-up of activity and then dies, with a lot of people left waiting for nothing."

Although the scheme was under investigation in the state of New York in the spring of 1987 and 17 suspects were actually arrested, it is difficult to prosecute the swindlers. For one thing, the initial promoters are long since gone by the time the authorities learn that a swindle is in progress. Then too, few victims are willing to come forward and identify themselves, not wishing to make their gullibility public knowledge and realizing that they have almost no chance of getting their money back.

On the Alert
For Pyramids

These five basic precautionary guidelines from the CBBB will help you avoid being exploited by pyramid scheme promoters.

---

1. Be wary if the start-up cost for the investment is substantial. Legitimate multilevel marketing companies usually require only a small start-up cost.

---

2. Find out if the company will buy back inventory. Keep it in mind that legitimate companies that require you to purchase an inventory should be willing to buy back at least 80 percent—in some states 90 percent—of what you paid.

---

3. Is there a consumer market for the products? If the company seems to be making its money by recruiting alone, stay away.

---

4. Before investing, get all the facts about the company, its officers, and its products. Get written copies of the marketing plan, sales literature, etc. Check with others who have had experience with the company and its products.

ALERT!

5. To check on a company, contact your local district attorney, state attorney general's office, or local Better Business Bureau. You may also want to contact the Direct Selling Association, a national trade association that represents legitimate in-home sales companies.

Chapter 10

TIME-SHARING OR TIME-SHAVING?

Time-sharing has been a boon to many families and couples who have invested their money in resorts that have been established and operated by responsible developers. The term "time-share" was borrowed from the computer industry, which coined it to describe a plan whereby many individuals from remote locations could gain simultaneous access to a central computer bank. In real estate, the term refers to the idea of joint ownership or rental of a vacation property—such as a condominium—by a number of persons, with each occupying the property for short periods of time. Participants thus can purchase one or two weeks in residence in a resort area at a cost far lower than that of year-round ownership.

The case of Jeremiah and Anne Newbury of Portland, Maine, is a good example. Having vacationed happily in Bermuda for 20 years, they were becoming increasingly dismayed at the escalating hotel costs, which had increased almost 70 percent in one five-year period alone. It looked for a while as though they were going to have to take their vacations elsewhere. But that was before they heard about time-sharing: investing with others in a resort property that could be shared on an annual rotating basis. On the recommendation of a friend, they visited a resort at St. George's Island that was in the process of converting to the time-share plan.

The Newburys knew the club as a cluster of white cottages in the oldest section of Bermuda. They had always loved St.

George's, known for its crooked streets, tiny alleyways with funny names like Petticoat Lane, Featherbed Alley, and Turkey Hill, and for its ancient forts and lighthouses.

They were almost reluctant to make the visit, fearing that this elegant historical section at the eastern end of Bermuda would be even more expensive than others. But time-sharing proved to be the answer and prompted them to make one of the best investments of their lives. For the sum of $8,100, they were guaranteed one week's occupancy each year for a period of 25 years in a handsomely appointed and furnished two-bedroom house that they have come to love.

"It was five years ago that we made the decision time-sharing was for us," says Jerry. "We've never regretted the investment."

Examples similar to the happy experience of the Newbury family can be cited in multitudes of choice locations from the Carolinas and Florida to the White Mountains of New Hampshire, the sun-drenched shores of California and Hawaii, and quite a few locations abroad. But for every glorious case history on record there is at least one that is tinged with problems ranging all the way from outright fraud and deception to mismanagement and lack of foresight.

Heads or Tails?

George and Susan Peterson had worked hard during 25 years of married life to acquire an attractive home and put their three children through school and college. Although vacations, sometimes in the form of motor trips and sometimes at a rented cottage by a lake or at the shore, had always been pleasant, the one thing they longed for was a second home in a permanent location. The dream had always eluded them because of tuitions, taxes, and other costs that took priority—that is, until they heard about the time-shares that were available in a resort community in their favorite state, Vermont.

Familiarizing themselves with the promises and implications of time-share terminology, they wondered why they had never known about or taken advantage of this pleasant kind of opportunity before. In essence, it all seemed quite simple: A relatively modest investment would buy them an actual piece of

one of the resort condominiums that was being built for occupancy the following year. They and the other co-owners
would take their turns using the property, which was adjacent
to areas available for swimming, sailing, golf, tennis, skiing, and
other forms of recreation that the Petersons enjoyed, both individually and as a family. The best part was that now they
would be established in a community that they could return
to and be a part of each year, rather than taking their chances,
helter-skelter, with whatever places were available at afford-
able rents.

Doing a little homework, George learned that time-sharing
was a $1.8 billion industry in the United States and that thou-
sands of families had already realized their vacation dreams
and were enjoying resorts that otherwise might not have been
economically feasible for them. Across America and around the
world, these property sharings took the form of condominiums,
apartments, single-family dwellings, and in some cases even
recreational vehicles, yachts, and houseboats.

For an investment of $18,000, George and Susan purchased
their Vermont time-share and looked forward to their first date
of occupancy in late 1985, when all five Petersons would enjoy
two weeks of skiing. In the meantime, they could have the plea-
sure of looking over the architect's plans and keeping abreast
of the progress of the construction. They might even take a
spin up to Vermont in mid-July, the time the condominiums
were to be finished, stay overnight at a motel, and explore the
nearby community and recreational facilities. George had already spent one day at the site in central Vermont, but that
had been long before any actual construction had begun.

The first hint of trouble came when the Petersons received
a memorandum that there was a "delay in the timetable." The
wording was vague but hinted that the promoters had decided
to hold up on one phase of the construction until they could
obtain "certain hardwoods of the durability we are demanding
for this top-quality facility."

Other indications of trouble followed in increasingly rapid
succession, the most frustrating being the inability to make
contact by phone or mail with the promoters or their salespeople. Finally, in desperation, George obtained an attorney

and demanded the return of his investment. By then, it was already too late. The promoters had filed for bankruptcy and the Petersons would be lucky to get back 50 cents on the dollar.

There you have both sides of the coin. But it would be a gross oversimplification to say that it is all a matter of luck whether the time-share investor flips heads or tails.

In the case of the Petersons, it turned out that the real-estate developer had good intentions but totally lacked experience in anything but the construction of tract houses, had poor financial counsel, and could not foresee the hidden costs that were eventually to cause the venture's downfall. You could call it "mismanagement."

Not so the case of an organization in Honolulu that touted its glorious promises under the alluring masthead "Paradise Palms Vacation Club." Starting in 1980, aggressive salespeople signed up more than 2,500 customers, selling shares with the assertion that the club was acquiring resort property in Hawaii and other choice locations where shareholders could select their annual vacation week. Prospective purchasers were shown sales brochures depicting elegant condominiums in Hawaii as the lure. What the brochures did not reveal was that the developer had only 20 units in Hawaii—enough for one out of five shareholders. Many people began to complain that it was impossible for them to schedule their annual vacation week in a condo in Hawaii, as they had been promised, and that the club pressured them into taking unacceptable substitute accommodations in places as far removed from Hawaii as apartments in Nevada or a motel in the state of Washington. Through deceitful promotion and outright falsehoods, the Paradise Palms Vacation Club turned out to be anything but what the name implied and went bankrupt, leaving its shareowners holding nothing but the bag.

Many such marketing abuses have been curbed, though unfortunately not eliminated. Even in Bermuda, where the government is unusually stringent about outlawing schemes that could tarnish the island's favorable image, things can sometimes go wrong. "Authorities are still stinging from adverse publicity about the Coral Island Club," said a recent report, referring to a hotel-conversion time-share that went broke in 1983. To the great good fortune of the individual investors, the bankrupt property was purchased by an insurance company as the site for a $20 million residential development, under an agreement to refund the money that otherwise would have been lost by the time-sharers.

Buying Time:
Pleasures and Perils

One of the most auspicious developments in the history of time-shares has been the entry into the business of large, reliable corporations. Their participation makes it more likely that investors will at least get their money back if the venture fails or they feel that they have been misled by the advertising and promotion that induced them to plunk down their money in the first place.

Large corporations engaged in time-share developments also have the back-up funds and clout necessary to obtain the kinds of choice sites that investors expect for their money, as well as the experience to estimate realistic maintenance and improvement costs over the period of time that purchasers have selected for their ownership. Equally important, reliable developers not only stand behind their promises but establish realistic timetables, so that shareholders can determine the availability of the residential units for the dates and locations desired. Many an otherwise acceptable development has lost face in the sometimes hectic shuffle to assign the preferred dates of occupancy.

The presence of large corporations and increasingly tougher state regulations has not altogether shut the door in the face of the quick-buck artists who ply their trade by exploiting the popularity of time-sharing. For example, in 1985 the Justice Department won a conviction that led to a three-year prison term for a man who had sold nonexistent time-shares in three states. Despite the fact that the conviction also included a $250,000 restitution judgment against the bogus company, many shareholders saw little hope of getting back more than just a small fraction of their investment.

Although the states that are most popular for time-share developments have by now established restrictions and laws to protect investors, clever con men can usually find ways of getting around, or evading, some of the regulations. Several years ago, hundreds of purchasers were attracted to a renovated Daytona Beach motel named Ocean Pointe when they visited an attractive model unit consisting of studio and kitchen. Expecting that this was what they would possess as a time-share, they were dismayed to arrive for their week's vacation to find that they had been assigned a damp, depressing room that had not seen a fresh coat of paint in years.

After they unsuccessfully demanded their money back (about $2,000 per time-share unit), they complained to the state of Florida. Only then was it discovered by state officials that the developer had never set up an escrow account, as the law required, to hold some $650,000 of the purchasers' money. It also turned out that the developer was already facing criminal charges in Michigan for having perpetrated a similar time-share fraud in Traverse City.

Despite the kinds of problems that have surfaced since time-sharing in real estate first became popular in Europe in the early 1960s, this kind of investment can be rewarding to families who are seeking not profits but attractive prepaid vacation accommodations at a reasonable cost. If you are interested in purchasing time-shares, your first responsibility to yourself is to learn just what you are getting for your money.

In a typical time-sharing program, an annual segment of time (usually one or two weeks) is made available for the use of a residential unit in a resort area that is desirable to the shareholder because of location and recreational opportunities. Prices range from a few thousand dollars to $20,000 or more to "own" a week or two of accommodations at a ski resort, beach condominium, mountain lodge, or similar vacation retreat. As might be expected, these prices depend on the quality of the accommodations and related facilities, the location, and the season. Generally, buyers make a down payment and pay the rest in installments, in such a way that the developer can finance the project over a period of many years without having to readjust the financial demands. Most shareholders are also committed to annual maintenance fees and the cost of a resort exchange program.

One recent development in the field is the time-share auction, for people who want to buy or sell their part-time vacation rights. At such sales, customers can often purchase "second-hand" shares at reduced prices, sometimes as much as 50 percent off the original price. At a recent auction, more than 80 bargain hunters bought time-shares at prices that ranged from $650 to $6,500, with an average price of $2,500. One auctioneer even has a catalog that lists unsold time-shares all over the world.

For those who want to combine the fun of owning their own vacation program with the savings of purchasing something substantial at a cost far less expensive than the price of a second home, the time-share market can offer a unique opportunity while posing a significant challenge.

The Two Basic Choices

There are two conventional types of time-share purchases, for which investors receive differing rights. The first is the *fee-simple,* which entitles the buyer to own a fraction of the residential unit selected. In essence, it is the same as getting together with a group of friends and buying a vacation home that will be used, in an agreed-upon rotation, by all.

You will be provided with a deed, along with rights to rent or sell your share of the property within whatever restrictions have been predetermined by the developer and mutually agreed-upon by the other purchasers. Under the fee-simple plan, you automatically join an owner's association, which will assume control of the resort from the developer once most of the units and available time segments have been sold—usually within two to four years of the time the resort has first gone on sale. In many cases, an owner's association will elect to retain the developer to manage the property, although it has the option of hiring an outside management firm.

The second type of time-share is called *right-to-use* and entitles the purchaser to use a residential unit for specified periods of time. The right-to-use plan grants occupancy rights for a specified number of years, perhaps as little as 5 or 10 or as many as 25 or 30. No deed is involved, but owners usually reserve the right to sell or lease their annual weeks, sometimes with necessary approvals.

Under a right-to-use agreement, the investor does not actually hold title to any property. Therefore, if the project is unsound and fails, the entire investment can be lost. But some states have now passed laws so that reimbursement funds are available to cover at least part of the loss.

Knowing the difference between the two basic types of investments is obviously vital before making any commitment, financial or otherwise. Although you want to take a positive outlook, thinking of a time-share in terms of vacations and recreational activities, it is only realistic to anticipate where you would stand in the event the development failed, the region became less attractive for vacations, or you eventually decided you would rather spend your holiday time somewhere else.

If you purchase a fee-simple time-share, it is important to know when your title becomes free of any claims by the financial institution that holds the property's mortgage. Usually that will not occur until a large percentage of time segments have been sold in your particular unit and until you have paid the developer in full.

If your contract is the right-to-use type, look for what is called a "nondisturbance" clause. This obligates the developer's mortgage holder or lender to recognize your occupancy rights in the event the property is foreclosed. The clause must not only be in your agreement with the developer but in the mortgage or construction loan granted to the developer by the financial institution involved.

Tips from the Experts

- Although time-shares often offer real-estate investment opportunities, think of them primarily as prepaid vacation facilities that offer you certain unique advantages.

- Plan to visit the site before you invest, not only to check out the property itself but to determine whether you really want to commit yourself to that location on specified weeks over a period of years.

- Be wary of any time-share developer who uses high-pressure tactics, offers all kinds of "free" prizes and incentives to attract prospects, and urges you to invest your money quickly before the units are sold out.

- Determine the nature of the long-term management, the practicality of the operating budget, and the maintenance fees you will have to pay now and in the future.

- Unless you are certain of the exact time and season of the year that you want to be in residence, find out whether there is a realistic plan for swapping dates of occupancy with other shareholders.

- Ask about the availability of exchange programs that would make it possible for you not only to change the dates of occupancy but to "trade up" to a larger or more elegant unit in the future.

- Make sure that your down payment is placed in an escrow account until your title to the unit is free and clear.

- Before you sign any contract for any time-share, no matter how reliable you know the developer to be, make sure that you understand each and every detail regarding your participation, rights, and options. When necessary, seek outside professional counsel.

ALERT!

- Before investing, make sure, through your own independent check, that the project is registered in its "state of domicile" with the Securities or Real-Estate Division of that state, and also make sure that it is registered for sale within your state.

- Investigate the whole network of properties under the time-share plan, not just the unit(s) in which you are specifically interested.

- Find out through local realtors what the asking prices are for vacation homes in the area that are comparable in size and comfort to the time-share units you have priced, and then compare the values carefully.

- Finally, make sure you really want to return to the area year after year and would not be doing so simply because you become locked into your purchase.

Chapter 11
THE COME-ON IN BONDS

A dealer in expensive recreational vehicles in the St. Louis area was enjoying a flush of prosperity in the fall of 1985, enticing prospective buyers by the hundreds with an advertising campaign he was running in local newspapers and airing in radio commercials. His pitch was pretty well summed up in this typical headline:

FREE!
A $5,000 U.S. TREASURY BOND,
FULLY GUARANTEED
WITH YOUR PURCHASE OF
ONE OF OUR NEW
DELUXE LAND CRUISERS

Among the eager buyers was a would-be entrepreneur who tried to talk his friends into pooling their resources and forming a sales syndicate. "If we buy ten vehicles and sell them at a $2,000 discount—a pretty good incentive—we'll still end up with ten $5,000 bonds, or a profit of $30,000."

What he did not know was that the $5,000 represented the maturity value of the bonds *30 years hence* and that each was purchased by the dealer at only a fraction of its face value, $200 to be exact. Fortunately for him, as well as quite a few other prospective purchasers who might have acted too hastily, state securities regulators banned further advertising of this kind by the dealer as "false and misleading." One local newspaper apologized in an editorial for having been duped by the advertiser and pointed out the difference between the high face value of the bond and the infinitely lower discount price paid by the dealer.

Duplicity Unbounded

Sales campaigns for houses, cars, and furniture based on the promotional use of zero-coupon bonds are misleading and purposely avoid telling would-be purchasers about potential disadvantages related to the securities that are touted as "bonuses." According to the North American Securities Administrators Association, "State securities regulators and Better Business Bureaus have observed a disturbing new trend in 'zero-based' sales campaigns, which frequently fail to inform customers of the current value of bonds, tax consequences, possible liquidity problems, and the extreme susceptibility to interest-rate fluctuations when 'zeros' are redeemed prior to maturity."

Purchases by investors in zero-coupon bonds have exceeded the astonishing sum of *$50 billion* a year during the past few years. In some instances, states have sharply restricted or have banned the use of "zeros" as a promotional device.

A typical example of this type of fraud was uncovered by the Alabama Securities Commission (ASC), which was investigating the methods used by an insurance salesman in Birmingham. It was disclosed that he had for two years participated in the purchase and redistribution of securities that were variously called not only zero-coupon bonds but "stripped treasury bond coupons," "treasury bond receipts," and "coupon treasury receipts." He had also been involved in the negotiation of letters of credit, utilizing these instruments as collateral.

The salesman was actively engaged in a scheme with a disbarred South Carolina attorney in which they operated a loan brokerage business in Columbia, South Carolina. Borrowers were required to purchase 10-year maturity securities with a maturity value equal to that of the requested loan. The attorney, upon obtaining an inflated price from the customer to purchase the securities, would then transfer the money to his Alabama partner, who was able to purchase the instruments at discounted prices from brokers in Arkansas and Tennessee.

The would-be borrower was led to believe that the amount he paid to the South Carolina partner in the scam was the actual cost of the securities, when in fact it was a great deal more than the going price. His judgment was blurred by his haste to get a loan at what looked like a real bargain rate by comparison with traditional methods. But the Securities Commission could find no evidence that any loans were ever closed once the victims had purchased the bonds. "This non-action on loan commitments," said the ASC, "left the customer with a 10-year maturity instrument that he could have purchased at a lesser price from a bank or securities broker himself."

One unfortunate case was that of a customer who was told that he could obtain a $500,000 loan by paying $200,000 for a bond that had a maturity value of $500,000. After he had made the purchase—with no loan ever forthcoming—he found that he could have purchased that same bond from any local bank for $120,000!

In another case, a customer was required to pay $600,000 to obtain securities with a value of $1,620,000 upon maturity. The Alabama partner made a profit of more than $70,000 and his South Carolina cohort more than $45,000, since they were able to purchase the bonds for less than $485,000.

Before the Securities Commission was able to halt the operations and expose the scam, the two men had managed to overcharge their customers by at least $520,000—all during a period of only 18 months.

"Repos" and "Junk Bonds"

It is ironic that bonds, which have long been considered very *conservative* financial instruments, have emerged as problem children in the world of swindles and scams. Perhaps the old-line reputation of bonds is what has made many investors unwary and willing to make purchases without question. Many fraudulent operations are intricate, difficult to track down, and challenging to prosecute. Where does "mismanagement" leave off and "fraud" begin?

In July 1987, the Securities and Exchange Commission (SEC) barred three former officials of the defunct Bevill, Bresler & Schulman firm from the securities industry. The chairman, former treasurer, and former executive vice president settled with the SEC without either admitting or denying allegations that they had engineered a complex fraud that cost scores of banks, thrifts, and municipalities about $150 million. They had already been convicted on criminal charges stemming from the fraud, which involved selling nonexistent securities, or the same securities to more than one customer.

"This was one of the largest securities frauds in history," said Thomas W. Greelish, the United States Attorney for New Jersey, describing a three-year-long scheme that ripped off the firm's customers while the three principals paid themselves more than $15 million in salaries, bonuses, fees, loans, and "disguised corporate payments."

The underlying scheme represents the kind of fraud you should be wary of in the purchase of bonds and other securities. According to an editorial in the *New York Times* of October 15, 1986, the fraudulent operations involved repurchase agreements, or "repos," under which the firm "sold government securities accompanied by agreements to repurchase the securities later by repaying the customer's purchase price, along with additional money as interest." The firm claimed that it would hold the securities in "safekeeping" accounts on behalf of customers for the duration of the agreement. However, according to the indictment, it "defrauded many customers by selling them nonexistent securities or securities that were supposed to be in safekeeping for others." Its woes started when it speculated heavily in bond futures and other high-risk investments and lost heavily. The only "out" was then to defraud its own customers.

"Junk bonds"—high-yield, low-rated, or nonrated bonds often associated with takeover bids—became a popular area of investment in the mid-1980s, inviting a good deal of financial loss on the part of investors who seemed to feel that they suddenly were able to get something for nothing. A "free lunch" was the way some critics described that incorrect perception of junk bonds, adding that very few things are really free these days and that too many investors are becoming convinced that they have found the formula for high returns at low risk.

"The junk bond vogue is new," said James Grant, editor of the *Interest Rate Observer,* "but there have always been shaky debtors and gullible lenders. More than a century ago, the Khedive of Egypt was borrowing not wisely but too well in London. In the 1880s, Argentina went broke, dragging along the illustrious banking house of Baring Brothers. In the 1890s, American railroad bond prices collapsed. In the 1920s, shiploads of bonds arrived in this country from foreign governments and municipalities. A fifth of them were in default by 1932."

Notwithstanding the high risks of some issues and the dramatic failures of others over the years, investors often seem to be oblivious to the financial weaknesses of some of the bonds they choose to invest in heavily. Mr. Grant cites, for example, junk bond issues whose prospectuses have carried, in print, such warnings as these:

"Based on current levels of operations and anticipated growth, the Company does not expect to be able to generate sufficient flow to make all the principal payments due on the Serial Senior Notes...."

"An investment in the Notes involves certain risks which prospective investors should carefully consider...."

"These risks include ... the insufficiency of the Company's earnings to cover fixed charges...."

"Notes will be subordinated and unsecured and will not be entitled to the benefit of any guarantees, unlike most of the Company's senior indebtedness."

The warnings on prospectuses for junk bonds (or any other types, for that matter) are required by law to provide important information to would-be investors. Yet it often seems that the investors are either oblivious to the warnings or overcome with a spirit of derring-do in the face of odds and risks. Why else, for example, would one note recently sell "briskly" at an enormously high price when the prospectus clearly stated that the issuing corporation had seasonal financial obligations that made it difficult, if not impossible, to come up with enough cash to service its indebtedness? Such puzzling behavior is due, perhaps, to sheer perversity on the part of investors who are not about to be discouraged by mere words.

Even the more cautious investor should be aware that, because most of these products are traded in the secondary market, investors will not get a prospectus. In such a case, don't hesitate to ask your broker for verified information.

Nowhere is the old adage "look before you leap" so important as in the consideration and purchase of bonds, where the value fluctuates with interest rates—whether they are junk bonds, zero-coupon bonds, or other instruments whose maturity dates stretch far into the future.

Zeros: Use and Abuse

Zero-coupon bonds, once described as "a backwater of the municipal bond market," became, after many years of relative obscurity, suddenly popular after President Reagan signed the sweeping tax-revision bill. They came into favor in part because some, such as municipal bonds, have certain tax-exempt features and because the low initial purchase price attracts investors who are saving for large future expenses, such as the education of their children.

But the very fact that "zeros" can be purchased at a steep discount from their face amount is what has made them the tools of con men and borderline promoters. When car dealers offer "free and tax-free" $5,000 bonds as gifts or bonuses with new car purchases, they are deliberately misleading prospective car buyers. For one thing, the tax-exempt claim may be open to question. More importantly, the dealers fail to disclose that the $5,000 "gift" actually cost them a mere $150 or so.

When these bonds are used to promote the sale of homes, an even riskier factor may be involved. The National Association

of Home Builders has warned that one common type of promotion, the use of zeros with face values equal to those of the
homes being purchased, could actually jeopardize the home-
owners' annual mortgage interest deductions or increase their
real-estate taxes.

Zero-coupon bonds are so named because there are no
semiannual coupon payments as there are with par bonds and
other securities. Zeros are automatically locked in at a specific
rate to achieve the stated yield. The advantage to investors is
that if they hold their bonds to maturity, they know exactly
what they will earn—but that is not the case if they want to
sell before maturity. The farther away the maturity date, the
lower the current selling price of the bond. For example, a $1,000
zero-coupon bond with an 11 percent yield might be purchased
for $330 if it has a 10-year maturity or for as little as $40 if it
will not mature for 30 years.

The Better Business Bureau advises that you remember that
a zero-coupon bond is an investment and should be treated as
such—not as a promotional device. These bonds are available
as corporate, municipal, or certificate-of-deposit offerings. They
vary widely in price, face amount, length of maturity, tax liability, and yield. Like other bonds, they also vary in the degree
of risk involved. Further complicating the decisions of would-
be investors is the fact that zeros are promoted under several
names, including Treasury Receipts (TRs), Certificates of Accrual on Treasury Securities (CATs), and Treasury Investment
Growth Receipts (TIGRs). They are all extremely susceptible
to shifts in interest rates when sold prior to maturity. What this
means in effect is that if you must sell a zero-coupon bond
prior to maturity, you run the risk of realizing much less than
you would with a coupon-bearing bond of the same maturity.

State securities administrators are constantly concerned that
sales promotions for these bonds often fail to inform customers
of this disadvantageous situation, leading them to believe that
they can make a killing any time they want to sell because of
the high face value of the instrument they have purchased.

When it comes to using them as promotional tools, one state
securities administrator summed up the situation this way: "The
retailers know zero about 'zeros.' The customers know zero
about 'zeros.' It's a nightmare situation for investor protection."

Be wary about any type of major purchase that promotes a deal whereby you will be given a zero-coupon bond as a bonus. Make sure you know—or get—the answers to these questions:

- What is the current market value, not the face value, of the bond offered, as paid by the promoter?

- How much could you purchase that same bond for through a reputable broker or bank?

- What are the tax consequences, in general, of accepting a bond as a gift, now or in the future?

- Could you make a better deal by purchasing a car (or home or other major item) whose incentive is something other than a bond?

ALERT!

- What is the resale market for the bond, should you want to sell before maturity?

- Does your state have regulatory restrictions that make this kind of "bonus" offer illegal?

- Is this a high-risk offering from an issuer who may not be able to pay the face value years hence when the bond reaches maturity?

There is no such thing as a "free lunch" when it comes to complicated securities, whether you buy them directly as investments or accept them as part of a promotional deal. As in the case of other securities, if you are considering a new issue, inquire about the bond's rating; find out what, if any, call provisions apply; and ask to see the prospectus, which will provide all the data you need to make a sensible decision.

Chapter 12

BOILER ROOMS

"Hello, Mr. Smith. How are you today?"

"I'm glad to hear that, because you're going to feel even better when I tell you about the government's big new land program in Montana. Have you read about it or heard about it on television?"

"I see. Well, that's because it's too new for most people to know about. But out here—I'm calling from Cody, Wyoming—we're all very excited about the big new opportunities for investment and future profits."

"I should explain who 'we' are. We're PLUS—Profitable Land Utilization Service—one of the gold-chip firms in the West. We work directly with the government in the sale of land to a limited list of customers who want to make sure they put their money only into sound, profitable investments. And what could be better than good land?"

"What has happened—and I'm sure you'll be hearing more and more about this—is that the United States Bureau of Land Management is being forced to auction off some of its most valuable properties in several national parks as part of the new deficit reduction package. We've been fortunate to acquire thousands of acres of rights and are offering choice sites as investments to our selected customers."

"Now, there's no commitment on your part, but if I can promise to show you some facts that could be very profitable to you, wouldn't you like to know how a very small investment at this time could at least quadruple your money in less than two years?"

"Now you're talking! I'll get some literature off to you in the very next mail out of Cody and let you see for yourself how really big the potential is...."

Reaching Out to "Touch" Someone

You are all too familiar with those irritating telephone solicitations for everything from storm windows to low-cost magazine subscriptions, bargain burglar-alarm systems, and elegant sets of simulated-leather bound encyclopedias at discount prices. Conditioned by experience to react with a decisive negative response to these persistent salespeople, you feel comfortably assured that you would never—absolutely not ever!—fall for a sales pitch aimed at getting you to put several thousand dollars into land or some other major investment. Or would you?

The unfortunate fact of the matter is that thousands of Americans who should know better are duped every year by smooth-talking salespeople operating out of small offices known as "boiler rooms." Playing on the listener's innate desire to get something for nothing or to parlay a small investment into a fortune overnight, they use clever dialogue and high-sounding terms to describe not only land but oil and gas leases, new-business opportunities, tax-avoidance partnerships, and other imaginative schemes that are very convincing. The lures always include assurances that you can take the next step with absolutely no commitments, see results quickly, and get your money back at any time if you are not satisfied with the deal.

Curiosity alone precipitates many victims into the action when they agree on the phone to look at the "literature." Before they know it, they get a second phone call, this time from someone who identifies himself as the manager of the firm or as a partner.

"One of my salesmen, Bob Jones, said he had talked with you and you might be interested in our big land opportunity in

Montana. Well, I've got exciting news for you because the acreage we obtained turned out to be on a lovely lake in the mountains and the choice site for a plush resort development. What we bought and can offer at a very low price will obviously go at premium prices. Right now, in fact, one of the biggest recreational developers in the West is starting to bid on the adjacent acreage. So we have to act fast!

"Did you receive our literature? Well, look at the map on page two and you'll see why I'm so excited about what we can offer our customers! We figure conservatively that an investment of only $5,000 would net you $25,000 or more in less than 18 months with no risk and. . . ."

The phrase "boiler rooms" originated in the 1920s when telephones were first used in the promoting of worthless stocks by groups of salesmen crammed into low-rent offices, which were described as being as hot as the area from which they derived their name. The term "bucket shops" has also been used for this kind of operation, but there is a small distinction. While boiler-room operators are engaged in the high-pressure peddling of stocks of dubious value, the bucket-shop operator actually accepts a client's money without ever buying or selling the securities the client orders. He simply pockets the money, gambling on the chance that the customer is wrong—when too many customers are right, he closes up shop and moves to a new location.

The art has become greatly refined in recent times, what with the installation of WATS lines to reach more prospects and the perfection of scripts that have been psychologically tailored to induce listeners to respond in a positive manner. The salespeople are well versed in ways to make themselves sound enthusiastic, sincere, honest, and credible.

Voice-switching is sometimes part of the act. The salesperson's pitch is suddenly interrupted by a supposed officer of the firm who implies that he simply cannot restrain himself from telling you about a brand-new development that can mean even more profits for investors. It is not unusual for some boiler-room promoters to make use of sound effects and other devices to heighten the excitement and give the listener the impression that his call is coming from a large Wall Street-type trading room where the action is going on at that very moment.

"In a rented room crammed with desks," reported *Business Week* in an editorial on boiler-room scams, "a dozen salesmen are on the telephone extolling the virtues of gold with evangelistic fervor to unseen customers. At the office manager's insistence, all of them stand when making a sales pitch. One man wears a gorilla suit. Another takes his motorcycle for a spin around the room, pushing the selling frenzy up a notch. They refer to written scripts to cajole or bully hesitant customers. Today they are pushing gold; tomorrow it could be diamonds, time-sharing condos, or penny stocks."

Long-Distance "Operators"

No one really knows the size or scope of boiler-room operations in the United States, since the firms have temporary offices, move frequently, and switch from one investment field to another, depending upon the popularity and allure of each market. It was estimated, however, that several years ago there might have been as many as 100 boiler rooms in Florida alone, employing some 2,000 salespeople around the clock. But the figures keep changing and the locations switching. California has also been a popular site for these fly-by-night operations.

The situation became so serious and the pressure from thousands of duped investors so great that Florida and California have been trying to stem the tide by controlling the activities of all firms that solicit customers by telephone, with the main thrust aimed at boiler-room operations.

Despite flagrant abuses of securities regulations and restrictions, however, the promoters of these schemes are very elusive targets for federal, state, and local authorities. "The perpetrators are a lot smarter than most people would like to believe," explained a director of securities in the office of the Florida comptroller's office. "They know how to fall between jurisdictional cracks—between criminal and civil, federal and state." They also know how to move fast, so that by the time the authorities are trying to indict them for land schemes, they have moved into precious metals or oil and gas, or have simply vanished from the scene.

Another major law-enforcement problem is that some of the firms that use questionable, high-pressure methods are headquartered outside the United States. These firms solicit by mail as well as through local salespeople in boiler rooms in various states. In December 1984, for example, the Dutch police raided an office in Amsterdam and confiscated the mail and equipment of a firm called Trier Investments, which was receiving an average of 80 check-containing airmail envelopes a day. Condemned as a "bucket shop," Trier was said to have cost its investors—many of them American—as much as $250 million for purchases of investments that were either hugely overvalued or were nonexistent.

Prospective American investors who might never fall for the pitches of boiler-room operators in their own country are fooled into thinking that the Dutch are the epitome of everything reliable and sound and would never resort to anything unethical. Unfortunately, reported the legal counsel of the Amsterdam Stock Exchange, over the past two or three years, "the country has been suffering from an invasion of shady dealers." Unregulated firms, "hiding behind polished brass plaques" along "Gentleman's Canal," the country's premier banking street, have been using bucket-shop techniques to push questionable investments. Among these have been worthless government bonds from Argentina, "odorless" coffee, and shares in a company reportedly putting wine in plastic bottles. Stock in one of these companies rose from $3 to $20 before the bottom dropped out and investors were left with nothing but paper.

One of the most successful categories for boiler-room operators is the oil and gas lottery. First of all, it lends itself to a very dramatic type of presentation, touting the discoveries of new petroleum fields that are sure to be big producers. Second, it calls attention to a fact that even schoolchildren are aware of by the time they have read American history books: numerous Americans, including farmers, small landowners, and inhabitants of Indian lands have become rich beyond their wildest dreams through the production of oil on property to which they held title. Third, since the government actually does conduct oil and gas lease lotteries, the promoters can use the legitimate news about such offerings as bait in follow-up phone calls to which they bring an air of breathless excitement.

Hook, Line, and Sucker

Why does a boiler-room operator select *you* as a hot prospect for his scam? He may have culled your name from the ranks of people who have inquired about legitimate stocks and other investments and whose names are thus computerized by firms that deal in sales lists. Or you may have stuck your neck out in the past by answering one of the promoter's own ads seeking people who would like to double their income or ensure themselves a worry-free retirement. Boiler rooms also exchange "sucker lists," knowing that people who get hooked on one scheme are likely to invest in another, as long as they can be reached before the awful truth dawns upon them.

A typical case was that of a commercial pilot in Oklahoma who sent in his check to purchase more than $7,000 worth of oil and gas lottery filings. Receiving a call from another salesman several months later, he coughed up almost $2,000 more for additional filings, even though he had not won a single government lease. He was kept on the string all that time by repeated assurances that "these things take time" and that he was without question going to obtain rights that would put him on the road to riches.

Some firms use gimmicks to solicit names, like offering a free handbook on investing or buying precious metals. They also imply that you have just been awarded a prize, which can be obtained by writing for further information. When you receive such literature, whose authors have pulled out all the stops to describe the pot of gold at the end of the rainbow, you will also most surely receive copies of valid news clippings describing the wealth of opportunities in whatever area of investment is being promoted. The idea is to make the fictional statements in the firm's brochure sound credible through false association with factual information.

Promoters do not hesitate to show you photographs of such subjects as "our staff geologist on location during recent exploration of the huge XYZ oil field in which we own a 50 percent interest" or "samples of high-yield ore from our uranium holdings in northern Mexico."

Individuals who are victimized need not berate themselves for being exceptionally stupid or negligent. Some of the biggest boiler-room scams have ripped off the most sophisticated bankers and major financial institutions. The Drysdale Government Securities scam is a case in point. Described as "one of the most complex cases of fraud ever to hit the arcane world of high finance," the scheme bilked one of New York's largest and most prestigious banks out of $270 million.

Drysdale Government Securities was formed in 1982 as a spin-off of an established Wall Street brokerage house that had been in business almost a century. Using two dozen traders who operated out of a fifth-floor room above a downtown clothing shop, the firm quickly amassed a portfolio of U.S. Treasury securities valued at more than $4 billion. The problem was that the promoters misrepresented themselves; first, by failing to mention that the securities were all borrowed, and second, by claiming to have more than $20 million in initial capital when, in fact, the firm was more than $190 million in the red.

Despite the falsifications, Drysdale Government Securities did business with the financial community, including several large banks, by generating capital from borrowed bonds. The house of cards collapsed when high interest rates drove bond prices down at a time when the promoters expected them to rise, making it impossible for the firm to pay back the $270 million it owed in interest payments and trading expenses. The firm's failure not only resulted in guilty pleas by the two indicted managers but also left a lot of red faces in the financial world—all of which is to say that small investors who are victimized can take a little consolation in the fact that they are not alone in their misery and embarrassment.

The Art Print Scam

One of the problems inherent in trying to protect the public is that investment scams cover a wide range of fields and are constantly changing. As people have become more and more interested in investing in art, for example, swindlers have raced to get into the act.

During the past few years, newspapers have headlined an increasing number of stories concerning works of art by noted masters that have escalated dramatically in value. The outcome of this publicity has been a rash of speculative purchasing by amateur art collectors who see this as a means of increasing their initial investments many times over. While few investors have aspirations of finding any bargains in Van Goghs or Cézannes, many are lured by opportunities to buy lithographs, engravings, and other fine-art prints by such celebrated artists as Salvador Dalí, Joan Miró, Pablo Picasso, and Marc Chagall.

Oft-publicized evidence shows that limited editions of prints by these popular artists have risen in value from $100 or less to several thousand dollars in just a few years. Where else could a person with cash on hand find such fortuitous circumstances for investment? One notable example was that of a lithograph by Jasper Johns entitled *0 Through 9.* Purchased in 1960 for a nominal sum by the Museum of Modern Art in New York City, it sold 25 years later for $93,500.

Even more aware of the profit potential than would-be collectors, however, have been the forgers, whose artisanship has been greatly enhanced by modern-day technology. Photomechanical techniques have made it possible today to transform high-quality color photographs of valuable works of art into lithographs or silk-screen prints that closely resemble the original works.

As a result, reported the *New York Times* in an editorial on fake art, "a network of art publishers and dealers in the United States and Europe is selling millions of dollars' worth of fake fine-art prints each year to would-be collectors around the country, according to leading auction houses, legitimate print dealers, and law-enforcement officials."

The counterfeits, usually represented as "original, handsigned, limited-edition prints," are worth at best $100 as reproductions. But the promoters demand prices well over $1,000 and sometimes as high as $8,000 if they get their hands on an eager amateur with visions of glory.

The fake-art scam has been around for centuries. But it really began to surface in a big way in the late 1970s, bolstered by dramatically rising art prices, improvements in copying techniques, and, of course, the increasing numbers of investors who began looking for places outside the conventional securities markets to put their money.

New York State's Attorney General Robert Abrams estimates that in recent years more than half a billion dollars has been paid by consumers for fake art in the U.S. alone. And, according to the International Foundation for Art Research, fake art prints represent the single largest facet of all art forgery swindles.

One reason fake prints have found their way into the world of high finance has been the discovery by the conventional, old-time swindler of that institution so well known to the securities business: the boiler room. Banks of telephones are manned by super-salesmen whose canned spiels are little different from those they formerly used to pitch worthless stocks and questionable land deals. Armed with lists of gullible prospects, they talk glowingly about the "chance of a lifetime" and urge their listeners to snap up the available Dalís and Picassos and Mirós before the opportunity is gone forever.

One of these pitches had a somewhat morbid twist. "As you know," the salesperson would say breathlessly, "Salvador Dalí is on his deathbed in Spain. Once he dies, the value of his work will jump like you couldn't believe. We have it from reliable sources that one of these prints we are offering you for $2,000 could go as high as $50,000! But you've got to act now or it will be too late."

One "art gallery" in New York, whose operators were convicted in a trial in 1987, was described by witnesses in court as "little more than a vestibule with several prints on the wall and two rooms with telephones." According to the testimony of an undercover agent who posed as a salesman, about 10 salespeople used the phones to solicit customers, but no prospective customers ever walked in.

Although the gallery gave a fancy "Certificate of Authenticity" to purchasers, one customer testified that he had three such certificates in his possession for what proved to be reproductions worth about one-thirtieth of the $7,000 he had paid for his purchases.

In another not-uncommon case, a doctor paid a total of $125,000 for 21 works that salesmen assured him were original, limited-edition lithographs. Their total worth was about $2,000. Over a period of several years, he had purchased them as part of an investment plan that he expected would provide him with a fine retirement fund. Yet he never once set foot in the gallery from which he made his purchases—all business was conducted by phone. By the time he tried to resell the art through Sotheby's auction house and discovered that he had been duped, the art gallery was long since out of business and the owners could not be traced.

Despite the hundreds of millions of dollars scooped in by swindlers and fly-by-night galleries, law-enforcement officials have been plagued by problems in trying to bring cases to court. For one thing, many victims are embarrassed at having been taken and avoid making charges or agreeing to provide testimony. Equally frustrating has been trying to determine exactly what is "original" and what is "fake."

"Definitions vary," said Rebecca Mullane, an assistant attorney general in New York. "And wherever there is an area of gray, it's a breeding ground for crooks. That's where the biggest frauds are, in unregulated areas where there is some degree of subjectivity in determining where the value is."

Forgers play on the confusion that exists even in the legitimate art world in determining whether a print is part of a "limited edition" (usually no more than 300) and whether a signature is real or copied. A major difficulty in obtaining a conviction lies in *proving* that the art dealer or wholesaler knew the works were not what was claimed. The standard defense by the retail dealer is that he relied on his wholesaler to supply works that were genuine. Then the wholesaler counters the charge by saying, "I supplied those as fine reproductions only. I didn't know the dealer was selling them as originals."

As the attorney general's office phrased it, the investigators found themselves constantly up against "a self-protecting circle formed to insulate its members from charges that they knowingly sold fakes."

If you decide to invest in art, don't do it over the phone. And even if you visit galleries that have all the trappings of authenticity, make sure you can take time to think about the purchase and that you have the opportunity to obtain an independent appraisal before you hand over your money. Be especially wary if a salesperson tries to pressure you to buy quickly, claiming, for example, that the artist is dying and the value of his works is ready to explode. The only thing that's failing may well be the wisdom of your purchase.

"Missionaries of Hype"

Still another problem facing agencies trying to protect the public is that there are no geographical limitations to many boiler-room operations. The very proficiency of con men and swindlers in the United States has resulted in what one financial editor referred to satirically as "America's hottest export—funny money stocks."

"Securities fraud is a skill developed to a high degree in the U.S.," he said. "Like missionaries of hype, North American con men, creeps, and hucksters who have fleeced Americans for years are currently spreading out across Europe, Asia, South America, and the Middle East. In the process they are repatriating at last some of the dollars left behind by free-spending American tourists and consumers. It's not an ideal way to redress our payments deficit, but it is making a lot of people rich."

These high-pressure salespeople, accustomed to at least a few restrictions and some investigative scrutiny in the States, find it ridiculously easy to operate their scams abroad, where securities laws and enforcement are virtually nonexistent. If they straddle national boundaries—using an office that is located in one country and pitching their sales to prospects in other countries—they stand an even greater chance of side-stepping the law.

Europeans are soft targets for boiler-room operators and the like, according to a German economist, because they tend to be less suspicious than Americans about a persuasive sales pitch. Then, too, they have read so much about the legends of American entrepreneurs who have struck it rich that they are willing to take a chance in order to achieve the same results. Con men abroad often open their pitch by touting the success stories of small U.S. companies that have reached the big time and have rewarded investors accordingly. Apple Computer is a popular and effective example. Thus, when the promoters mention the stock issue they are offering in a bogus or marginal company, the prospect begins to have visions of riding its coat-tails to glory—just as some investors have done with real-life corporate winners.

An investigator for Interpol estimated that in a single year, the six largest boiler rooms run by Americans in Amsterdam alone skimmed $200 million from Europeans. "That's just one city and only six operators out of a score," he pointed out. "The total losses could surpass $1 billion. Quite a haul!"

Among the types of bogus investment "opportunities" promoted by boiler rooms in Europe have been Sundance Gold Mining & Exploration, Inc., described in a *Forbes* report as "worthless"; North American Bingo, which was a shell without even an office typewriter and which went from 10¢ to $2.50 on paper; Swissoil, which attracted buyers who were told that there was plenty of oil under the Alps; and what was described as "one of the most outrageous hustles," a company called Derby-Vision that was supposedly marketing a slot machine for betting on horse races. Many of these penny-stock companies are ones that have already been exposed, outliving their usefulness in securities scams in the United States, and so have been revived for the European trade.

As for the cast of characters on the European scene, it is composed of the usual seamy bunch of folk found in any typical boiler-room operation. Among the recent promoters, as reported in an article in *Forbes* magazine in the fall of 1985, were Tommy Quinn, then living in luxury in the south of France but once a resident of the federal penitentiary at Danbury, Connecticut, where he served time for stock fraud; Barry Marlin, who had among his credentials a 10-year prison sentence for running a $40 million Ponzi scheme in California; and David T. Winchell, Canada's "most notorious white-collar criminal," who once had to pay $1.6 million in fines to avoid two years behind bars for looting a public corporation.

With talent like this masterminding boiler rooms, is it any wonder that many an otherwise astute investor falls prey to heady dialogue and the lure of financial adventure?

Two former salesmen once described the kinds of techniques used to motivate them to rip off ever-larger quotas of prospects over the telephone. One was to pin $500 in bills on the boiler-room wall, right over the bank of phones. The prize went to the salesman who produced the largest number of customers that day. Other incentives were Cadillacs and luxury vacation trips. "That hustler," said one disgruntled victim of the salesman who snared him, "could sell parking tickets to a judge!"

"Hello, Mr. Smith. How are you today?"

"Fine. That's just fine. Now for the good news. I'm calling about the geological data I sent you on PDQ Treasure Mines, Ltd. Well, you can *double* the production figures. I've just come back from a visit to our holdings in northern Saskatchewan and you wouldn't believe the way those chaps up there are panning the gold...."

Breaking the
Boiler-Room Connection

Whenever you receive telephone calls offering any form of investment "opportunity," whether unsolicited or in answer to a request for information, be sure to check out the following basic information.

- *Registration.* Ask whether the offering is filed with the state securities commission or any other official body controlling such matters. Find out exactly which agency you should contact to confirm the offering.

- *Salespeople or Principals.* Obtain the names, addresses, and phone numbers of anyone you talk to on the phone who is making the offering. Ask what their background is in the field in which the investment is being offered and why they have particular interest in this venture.

- *The Company.* Request background data about the firm offering the investment opportunity, preferably in the form of a prospectus or offering document. If the subject is technical in nature, request information about the firm's track record in past investments in the field.

- *The Commission.* Make sure you have a clear understanding of the commissions and/or other compensation the firm will receive if you do make an investment.

- *Escrow Holdings.* Make sure that investors' funds are kept in a separate escrow account where they cannot possibly be commingled with other funds or withdrawn by any of the firm's officers.

ALERT!

- *The Investment Itself.* Request a prospectus or other acceptable document describing the exact nature of the company and operations involved and the nature of the risks and potential. In the case of an offering that relates to natural resources (petroleum, precious metals, land, etc.) make sure you obtain reliable reports from geologists or other specialists qualified to render such judgments.

- *Taxes and Other Assessments.* Make certain you have an accurate understanding of elements and operations that will affect your tax obligations, short-term or for the future.

Under no circumstances should you part with any money or make any commitments until you have all the necessary data and documents in hand. In case of any doubt, call or write the office of your state Securities Division or your local Better Business Bureau, or consult with a specialist who can provide reliable counsel.

Take a minute to review the "Ten Do's and Don'ts for Investors" found at the end of chapter 1. And remember, whether an investment offer comes to you through a personal solicitation, by mail, or over the phone, *if it sounds too good to be true, it probably is.*

Chapter 13

HOW TO SELECT AND DEAL WITH A STOCKBROKER

ALERT!

The situation was quite commonplace, the result of an everyday occurrence found in large cities and small towns across the face of America. An elderly lady was widowed. After the estate had been settled and the life insurance paid, she found that she had $200,000 in the bank to see her through her declining years. Her relatives urged her to invest in securities so that she could live on the proceeds from her investments and not have to dip into capital.

After listening to suggestions from her peers, women who had found themselves in similar circumstances, she visited the offices of a local stockbroker and sought his guidance. With a sound financial program under way, everything seemed to be going fine. She had a healthy balance of growth and income and felt comfortable in the hands of a stockbroker who seemed to be both reputable and professional. In fact, when the broker decided to move to another firm, she agreed to transfer her entire account with him.

That is when her troubles began.

Adhering to industry policy, her broker was required to complete a new-account form before he could open up the account. In filling the form out, he altered the widow's designated investment objectives, without her knowledge or consent, in a way that gave his firm approval for trading in all kinds of options. The widow had orally authorized the broker to exercise discretion in her account, as long as he acted in accordance with her investment objectives, which heretofore had been conservative. Instead, the broker went on what one securities regulator described as a "commission-generating rampage," completing more than 170 trades in the course of a single year.

While the broker realized commissions of almost $70,000, the net loss to his customer's account was close to $35,000. It was a classic case of "churning," excessive trading by a broker to make more in commissions while disregarding the best interests of the customer. The widow, disillusioned and deeply disgusted by the lack of honor in a profession she had assumed was above reproach, brought legal action against the broker and his firm. She received $54,000 in settlement and had the satisfaction of seeing the broker barred from stock exchange membership.

Unfortunately, as recent scandals on Wall Street have revealed, individual stockbrokers are just as susceptible to dishonesty and prone to mismanagement as are any professionals responsible for handling large sums of money as part of their job. As case after case documents, the temptation to indulge in excessive trading is only too common, along with the urge to "borrow" sums from a customer's account in order to use inside information to speculate in the market.

Needless to say, stockbrokers are subject to the same human failures as everyone else. Even the most conscientious broker will be unable to meet your expectations 100 percent and may even make unfavorable decisions that affect the value of your portfolio. "But, given the necessary concessions to the realities of living in an imperfect world," says Stephen C. Schuyler, supervisor of enforcement of the Securities Division of the state of Maine, "there are many things you can do to increase your chances of establishing a good relationship with a stockbroker, which in turn will increase the likelihood of realizing your ultimate investment goals. The process of attaining such a relationship can be summed up in one sentence: Know *yourself,* know the *broker,* and know the *investment alternatives.*"

Establishing Your Goals

More than 42 million Americans from all walks of life own shares in the nation's businesses. A New York Stock Exchange survey revealed that 40 percent of these investors had annual incomes under $25,000. Since investing is a complex function, even for those who decide to undertake it in modest fashion, the guidance of an experienced stockbroker or other financial specialist is usually essential in order to achieve success in the stock market. How, then, do you choose and deal with a stockbroker, also known as an "account executive" or "registered representative"?

The first step, before you try to select a brokerage firm or an individual broker, is to determine as realistically as possible your financial needs and investment objectives. Are you seeking *long-term growth, a steady income flow, tax savings, quick profits*—or a combination of these? The best way to reach a decision is to review your personal finances. If you enjoy a good income or are relatively young and can handle a degree of risk in order to seek larger gains down the road, your goal might well be growth through the appreciation of capital. Conversely, if you are living on a fixed income, your objective should be to protect your capital while bringing in modest income through dividends and interest.

Start with the premise that *no investment is risk free* and keep this in mind whenever you take money out of one pocket to put it in another. As a general rule, the greater the hoped-for return, the riskier the investment. Never make any investment unless you have sufficient cash reserves to cover personal emergencies and unless you have adequate life and health insurance. Even substantial assets, however, are no guarantee that each investment opportunity that appeals to you will be appropriate or compatible with your goals.

Having made an honest and realistic appraisal of your monetary situation, you will do yourself a favor if you check the data and figures with an accountant or someone familiar with your financial status. If you are married, by all means let your spouse share directly in the evaluation and planning. The same is true if there is an interdependence between you and parents, adult children, or other close relatives whose financial circumstances are tied in with your own.

Only now are you ready to seek out the stockbroker who will best serve your interests and understand your goals.

Selection and Guidance

Stockbrokers fall into two basic categories, one offering full service and the other offering a discount. The full-service broker recommends specific stocks or investment strategies tailored to your financial needs and the size of your account. Commissions are paid based on the number and size of transactions made in your account. The discount broker makes transactions on your behalf at a lower commission rate but generally does not recommend specific securities or strategies. Of course, there is no reason you cannot use two brokers, one offering full service and the other offering to make transactions at a discount.

Brokerage relationships are highly personal and the nature of the service you receive will depend not only on the firm but on the account executive you select. Many people feel comfortable asking for recommendations from friends, business associates, or professional people they know and trust. A recommendation, however, is no guarantee that what is right for them is also right for you. That you can judge only after you have read brochures from several likely firms, studied the descriptions of services provided, and talked with the local office managers. If they understand your investment goals and appear receptive, they will turn you over to a broker who is knowledgeable about your areas of interest.

Now, at last, you find yourself face-to-face with the person who may become your very own broker. "When you meet with a particular broker at the firm, treat the occasion as an interview," advises an investment newsletter. "Don't be intimidated by an impressive office or a fast-paced, smooth but superficial sales pitch. Discuss your investment goals and financial capabilities fully with the broker. Ask questions and listen to the answers you get. Remember, there are no dumb or silly questions when it comes to understanding how your hard-earned money is going to be invested."

You are the only one who can then judge whether the firm's services, commission structure, approach to guidance, and "personality" are compatible with your own objectives. Once you select a broker, he will ask for data to fill out the required new-account form. Among other things, you may be asked questions about income, net worth, taxes, and past experience with investments. You most certainly will want to provide as much information as possible about your objectives, the degree of risk you can or cannot take, and the options you will leave in the hands of your broker. Don't take offense at any questions that seem to pry into your affairs. For your own protection, brokers are *required* to know their customers. Keep in mind, too, that if your financial situation or objectives should change in the future, you must be sure to keep your broker informed of the changes.

Additional forms and personal files are required if an investor desires certain services. These services include buying securities with money borrowed from your broker at interest, a practice known as buying "on margin"; trading in options or commodities, which are volatile and risky; and allowing your account executive to act on his or her discretion without obtaining your permission.

Just because you have selected a broker in whom you have confidence does not mean that you can now turn your back on your investments and let the account representative handle the details. A wise investor is an *informed* investor, one who studies the market regularly and can ask a broker intelligent questions about various securities. This is increasingly important in light of the numerous and complex financial instruments being offered today. One good source of data will in all likelihood be newsletters and other publications that are mailed to you by the broker or that can be obtained on request from the firm's research department. The subjects of these range from new investment opportunities to market trends, tax revisions, and other pertinent matters.

When brokers recommend a security, they should do so not on the basis of "hunches" or "tips" but on sound reasoning and substantial grounds for believing that the investment is suitable from the standpoint of the customer's objectives, financial situation, and current needs. Always ask your broker to supply copies of the research or other data used as a basis for evaluating a specific security. Brokers are not hesitant in any way about supplying this kind of information since they realize—as you should also—that good and continuing communications are vital between brokers and their customers.

The frequency with which your broker calls you to make recommendations should be consistent with your investment objectives and the size and value of your portfolio. For example, if you hold only five or six securities and they are invested for long-term, conservative growth, there may be no need for you to talk to your broker more than once or twice a year. However, a larger account which includes a number of highly speculative stocks requires constant and vigilant attention. In this case, a broker may phone several times a week.

If you own stock in publicly held corporations, it is essential that you read the annual reports and quarterly or other periodic statements of the companies in question. You can also obtain such reports, directly or through your broker, from companies in which you might want to purchase shares, even if you are not a stockholder. There are also numerous business periodicals and financial services to which you may subscribe.

When Something Goes Wrong

What do you do and where do you turn if you have problems with your account or your broker? First, you have to try to determine where the fault lies. Some investors simply expect too much from brokers, as though they possessed hidden powers of insight which they were not sharing. Clairvoyance exists in the investment field mainly in hindsight, and it is all too easy to decide, after the fact, what should have been done. Other investors run into problems because they have not presented their needs and goals clearly enough or have indulged in a lot of wishful thinking when imparting their financial dreams to their brokers.

Real problems do arise, however, even when the initial communication has been clear and the goals mutually recognized. Some of these problems are functional, such as the late delivery of a stock certificate or dividend check. Other problems may

be more serious, involving sales practices that have weakened your control of the account and muddled the objectives. One of the most common and debilitating problems is the matter described earlier: churning, or excessive trading. Equally disruptive are unauthorized buying and selling of securities, selling investment products to investors for whom they are not suitable, and the failure to execute trades desired by a customer or to deliver securities.

Whenever you detect a problem or are skeptical about a practice or procedure, contact your account executive as quickly as possible. If the representative is away, ill, on vacation, otherwise unavailable, or uncooperative, speak to the manager. In the investment field, speed is always essential and delay can be costly. It is important, too, to have readily available all recent statements from your brokerage firm so that you can verify— or question—any transactions about which you have reservations or doubts.

If a security has been bought or sold erroneously through a misunderstanding, the chances are that the broker can rectify the mistake without much difficulty. If you delay too long, however, you place yourself in a "wait-and-see" situation in which it could logically be inferred that you wanted to determine what the results of the action might be before making a complaint.

What if you speak to both your broker and the office manager and still have not resolved the problem or received what you feel is a straight answer? Your next recourse is to the chief compliance officer at the firm's home office, whose name must be given to you on request. If you still do not get a satisfactory response, phone or write the office of the securities commissioner in your state. Other sources of action and information are the regional offices of the United States Securities and Exchange Commission, the National Association of Securities Dealers, the National Futures Association, the Commodity Futures Trading Commission, and the various stock exchanges.

If all else fails and you still feel that you have lost investment money through no fault of your own, you may wish to consider legal action or arbitration. An arbitration claim is a method of resolving a dispute between two parties through the intervention of a third, impartial party knowledgeable in the area of controversy. Arbitration offers a less costly and generally faster means of settlement than conventional lawsuits and litigation. It is vital for you to understand, however, that arbitration awards are *final*. By selecting arbitration as a means of resolving a dispute, you effectively forego your right to pursue the matter through the courts should the decision go against you.

The chances are good that if you follow the basic suggestions outlined earlier about establishing your investment goals and selecting a broker, you will never be in the position of having to take legal action or seek arbitration. Be an informed and aware investor, alert to changes in the market and those economic trends that shape the course of the money world. Never hesitate to ask questions of your broker and don't be afraid or embarrassed to say "no" to any recommendation you feel is off target. No reputable broker will try to twist your arm or overrule your judgment.

And bear in mind at all times that *no investment is risk free, and the greater the profit potential, the greater the risk.*

For a Better Broker Relationship

Compatibility, communication, confidence, and peace of mind are all essential when it comes to putting your money—and your future—in the hands of a professional. Here are some points to check to ensure that you are in good hands and aiming in the right direction.

- Find out whether the brokerage firm you have selected is a member of any recognized national stock exchange or of the National Association of Securities Dealers and the Securities Investor Protection Corporation.

- Before dealing with any broker's office, you might consider contacting your state securities commissioner or local Better Business Bureau to verify that the firm and broker are duly licensed in your state and to learn whether either has been disciplined by any regulatory agency.

- In order to communicate better with your broker, read a booklet that will help you interpret the data contained in annual reports. Write the American Institute of Certified Public Accountants, 1211 Avenue of the Americas, New York, NY 10036, and ask for *What Else Financial Statements Can Tell Me.*

- Never buy on the basis of rumors or so-called "hot tips." Keep your eyes open, act on fact rather than emotion, and if the urge gets out of hand, call your broker and ask for a research report on the security you have in mind.

- If you feel uncomfortable with your brokerage house or account executive, or have reason to feel that you are being pressured in any way, don't feel guilty about switching your account to another representative or firm. After all, your financial future is the one at stake—not theirs.

Conclusion

"The American public is better educated and better informed than ever. But here's a paradox: The more people know, the dumber and more careless they seem to get about their investments."

That statement set the tone in an article in *Forbes* magazine in the spring of 1985 entitled "The Smarter They Are, The Harder They Fall." Since that time, despite warnings galore from Better Business Bureaus, state and federal regulatory agencies, and the nation's press, that sorry fact has been borne out again and again—as has been true for generations. And the scams and rip-offs you have read about in this book will continue to be repeated in substance for generations to come, with only the names and come-ons revised to tie in with current trends and activities.

Are the con men whose specialty is parlaying fraudulent tax shelters into big business discouraged by the fact that the new tax laws have all but eliminated this form of financial advantage to big investors? Quite the contrary. All they have to do is dream up imaginative but plausible "loopholes" to snare a fine new string of ready suckers. Already a number of new tax shelter schemes have been detected, suggesting that this may be a profitable field again for the promoters who prey on individuals looking for easy ways to beat the IRS.

Yet tax shelters have been only a small part of the game, by comparison with the multitude of other schemes. Even the major investment frauds that make headlines week after week are modest when stacked up against the millions upon millions of dollars lost by middle-class, small-town investors, and senior citizens bilked out of hard-earned pensions and retirement savings. Ironically, most of the victims are neither dumb nor ill-informed. Not uncommon is the recent case of a very capable and respected businesswoman who died in her early seventies. Close relatives, estimating that her estate would be worth at least $500,000, were shocked when informed by her attorney that the only things of value left behind were a modest home and some jewelry. All of her many investments turned out to be practically worthless pieces of paper—sad testimony to the fact that she had been duped into buying stocks that were either highly misrepresented or fraudulent.

It is surely too easy to speculate on dreams only to discover too late that some stocks have nothing more than a fanciful story behind their performance. Promoters tout these high-flying stocks as the next Xerox or IBM, a venture starting on a shoe-string and aimed at the heavens. Very often, unfortunately, there is no substance behind the exciting lure, some marvelous new product or service that promises to mushroom into high earnings and a bright future. Those in the know, however, refer to such ventures as "puff stocks" and warn investors that it is better to do some cautious investigating first, rather than leaping to "get in on the ground floor." The late 1980s has seen a steady stream of puff stocks, all with direct tie-ins to current events and with seemingly great potential. The products touted have included wonder drugs for AIDS, wrinkle-erasing skin creams, a revolutionary new type of internal combustion engine, wristwatch beepers, and technological systems for improving visual communications. Many of the companies promoting these "exciting new developments" may have market values of from $100 million to $800 million yet be unable to document more than $1 million or $2 million in annual sales.

Not all such companies are fraudulent, and a very few do manage to survive and prove valuable to early investors. But most are the subject of overpromotion and boiler-room tactics on the part of the broker-dealers engaged in selling their stock.

Congratulations—
It's Your Lucky Day!

You've just received a letter or telegram informing you that you have won a deluxe vacation for two, a free weekend at a resort, a fabulous diamond brooch, or a high-tech stereo system. Good news? According to the Council of Better Business Bureaus, member Bureaus across the country have been receiving a growing number of complaints about promotions based on phony prizes and deceptively advertised prices. The gimmick was once used mainly as an inducement to get prospective buyers to look at real estate or purchase relatively low-priced merchandise.

But the trend has been to promote much larger investments, often involving contractual agreements that cannot easily be dissolved by consumers once they find they have been lured into something they never anticipated. The "lucky day" is more often for the promoter, not the buyer.

Another trend that will most certainly continue is the use of the names of well-known people to make prospective investors feel more secure. One example is "Culture Farms," which was more earthily described by government regulators as "crud farms." The idea apparently originated in South Africa, where investors reportedly were taken for about $50 million. Before the scheme was restricted in the United States, thousands of people had lost an estimated $10 million by paying $350 each for packages of a "magic" powder that supposedly would double in value when mixed with milk and cheese and left to "mature" in jars. The resultant glop, it was claimed, was the basic ingredient for a new line of cosmetics called "Cleopatra's Secret." The only "secret" was that no one would buy the rotting mixture for any price, and the investors, many of whom ordered large quantities of the powder, were left holding the bag—or the goo, if you will.

"Culture Farms," reported *Forbes* magazine when the scam was publicized, "used an unwary actress, the wholesome Jane Powell, to lend credibility." When reporters asked Powell's agent if he was aware that the promoter was being investigated by state securities regulators, he replied, "Good God, no!"

In some cases, well-known figures are themselves the pro-moters. In August 1987, the *New York Times* reported on the case of Glenn W. Turner, who had just been sentenced to seven years in prison for fraud. Turner, founder of the popular "Dare to Be Great" motivational program, had been taken to court for promoting an Arizona-based scheme to defraud people of thousands of dollars. He and two other men were accused of falsely promising investors incomes of $1,000 to $3,000 a month if they would invest an initial outlay of $5,000 in a company called Challenge, Inc., which proved to be nothing but a pyra-mid scheme.

One noticeable trend in investment frauds in recent years has been what might be called the "internationalization" of scams and schemes that formerly were confined to the United States or were regional in nature. Often, when U.S. regulatory agencies crack down on fraudulent operations at home, the con men simply move operations to foreign shores, sometimes with little danger of being hauled into court. The United States Securities and Exchange Commission has become so concerned about this trend that it has expanded its operations to include agreements with other countries in an attempt to get more help from overseas in putting a lid on securities frauds. At a pace-setting meeting in Paris in the summer of 1986, members of the International Organization of Securities Commissions and Sim-ilar Agencies met to discuss this kind of cooperation. It was admitted, however, that such efforts and measures were in their earliest stages.

Whether such cooperation will be effective in impeding in-ternational fraud remains to be seen. Soon after that Paris meeting, investigators in New York City uncovered a swindle involving fraudulent Indonesian government promissory notes with a face value of $3.5 *billion.* They reported their belief that the scheme was controlled by a Middle Eastern businessman linked to the Palestine Liberation Organization. Five European traders were subsequently indicted on charges of trying to sell $640 million of the notes to an undercover police detective. "In dollar amount, it's staggering," said Richard Ward, the special agent in charge at the Secret Service in New York. "But it's really just a big scam."

The size of many a fraudulent international operation is indeed astonishing, and the implications are frightening. Individuals who invest in such schemes may not only lose their money but may eventually discover that they have helped to support foreign groups—even terrorist organizations—in a way that was certainly never their intent.

What further worries regulators in the United States is that there is a tremendous amount of "talent" overseas that is evidently not going begging. What has happened to the likes of Marc Rich, the infamous master of commodities and futures trading fraud, who fled to Switzerland and then Spain while facing 51 separate criminal charges; Pincus Green, indicted in 1983 for evading $48 million in taxes, who escaped to Switzerland; elusive Robert Vesco, who swindled investors out of $224 million before seeking shelter in South America and then eventually in Cuba; or P. Takis Veliotis, a former senior executive at General Dynamics who is now on the lam in Greece after being charged with taking kickbacks of $1.3 million?

You had better believe that many such outcasts who were caught with their hands in the cookie jar are behind imaginative and fraudulent schemes to bilk still more investors out of their money, one way or another.

Three thousand years ago, King Solomon proclaimed that there is nothing new under the sun. He might as well have been speaking about investment frauds today. Behind almost every scheme, there is a long history of similar scams. The problem, of course, is that they are so cleverly camouflaged that they seem to be *new* opportunities—ways to make a buck without breaking one's back. What happened to all the victims described in this book could happen to almost anyone who invests without taking the time to investigate.

Glossary of Terms

Abusive tax shelters. Fraudulent schemes for avoiding taxes through investment programs which supposedly allow certain deductions but which, in effect, are illegal.

Account. A broker's record of his customer's transactions; bookkeeping records in general.

Account executive. A broker or salesperson responsible for a customer's securities transactions.

Annual report. A formal statement issued yearly by a corporation to its shareholders. It shows assets, liabilities, equity, revenues, expenses, and so forth, and is a reflection of the corporation's condition at the close of the business year.

Antifraud provisions. Federal and state securities law provisions imposing liability for, among other things, omission or misstatement of fact in the purchase or sale of securities.

Arbitrage. Buying a stock in one market and simultaneously selling it in another, to take advantage of a price differential between the two markets.

Arbitration. A system for resolving disputes under which two parties submit their disagreement to an impartial panel for resolution. Decisions of an arbitration panel are binding on the parties to the claim.

Assets. Everything of value that a company owns or has due.

Beneficial owner. The owner of securities who receives all the benefits, even though the securities may be registered in another name.

Bid-and-asked quotations. The "bid" is the highest price offered for a security at a given time, while the "asked" is the lowest price anyone will accept at that time.

Blue chip. Common stock in a company known nationally for the quality and wide acceptance of its products or services, and for its ability to make money and pay dividends.

Blue sky laws. Laws enacted by various states which may require the registration of securities and securities agents, and which protect the public against securities frauds.

Boiler room. A temporary office equipped with phones from which banks of salespeople call lists of prospects in the hope of talking them into purchasing worthless or greatly overpriced securities or other investments.

Broker. An agent, often a member of a stock exchange firm, who handles the public's orders to buy and sell securities and commodities, for which service he charges a commission.

Broker-dealer. Any person engaged in the business of offering or selling securities for his own account or the accounts of others.

Churning. Excessive trading of a customer's account by a broker who has control over the trading decisions and whose purpose is to increase commissions without heeding the best interests of the customer.

Commission. A broker's fee for handling transactions in an agency capacity.

Commodity. An article of commerce in which contracts for future delivery may be traded. Among the most common commodities are corn, cotton, livestock, copper, gold, silver, petroleum, currency, Treasury bills, and bonds.

Debit balance. Situation in which the trading losses in a customer's account exceed the amount of equity in the account.

Delayed delivery contract. A contract for the purchase or sale of securities or commodities to be delivered at an agreed future date.

Discretionary account. A securities account operated with the customer's consent allowing the broker or dealer to trade without prior approval.

Dry hole. A completed well which is not productive of oil and/or gas in commercial quantities.

Due diligence. Careful investigation by a broker-dealer, necessary to ensure that all information pertinent to an issue has been disclosed to the public.

Face value. The redemption value of a bond or preferred stock appearing on the face of the certificate. Also called "par value."

FDIC. Federal Deposit Insurance Corporation, an agency of the federal government created to guarantee bank deposits.

Fiduciary duty. The legal and moral responsibility of brokers to act responsibly and with special care in the handling of their customers' accounts.

Forward contract. A transaction in which the buyer and seller of a commodity agree upon delivery of a specified quantity and quality of the commodity at a specified future date.

Franchise. A special privilege granted to an individual or group willing to invest a specified sum in order to obtain the right to market products or services under the name of the corporation selling the franchise.

Futures contract. A firm commitment to receive or deliver a specified quantity and grade of a commodity during a designated period of time, with the price determined by public auction among exchange members.

Hot issue. A public offering where securities, after their initial sale to the public, are resold in the open market at prices substantially higher than that of the original public offering.

Issue. A series or class of securities which has been or is being sold by a company; the marketing and distributing of a new class or type of securities.

Kiting. A scheme to obtain an unauthorized and unsecured bank loan without interest charges. The scheme is based on the fact that a check deposited in one bank is not instantly recorded as a withdrawal from the bank account upon which it is drawn. During the one- to four-day delay, checks can be cashed against the apparent balance.

Leverage contract. A standardized agreement calling for delivery of a commodity, with payments against the total cost spread out over a term of years. This form of agreement is also commonly known to the trade as a "margin account" or "leverage account."

Manipulation. The illegal practice of buying or selling securities for the purpose of creating a false appearance of active trading or raising or depressing the price to induce purchases or sales by others.

Margin deposit. The amount of money or other collateral deposited to insure a broker or clearinghouse against loss on futures contracts.

Maturity. The date on which a loan, bond, or debenture comes due.

Misappropriation. The unauthorized use of, or interference with, the right of ownership over money, investments, or property.

Misrepresentation. False or misleading statements relied upon by a customer making decisions to trade commodities futures, options, or other securities.

NASD. National Association of Securities Dealers, one of whose functions is to enforce rules of fair practice and prevent fraudulent and manipulative acts.

Nondisclosure. Failure to disclose key facts needed by the customer to make decisions about trading in securities or other investments.

Odd lot. An amount of stock less than the normal 100-share unit of trading.

Option. A trading tool used in commerce, which gives the buyer the right to buy or sell a quantity of a commodity or security at a specific prearranged price within a specified time period, regardless of the market price of the commodity at that time.

Over-the-counter (OTC). A market, mainly conducted through the phone and computer networks, in which securities not listed on a national exchange are traded. The market includes government and municipal bonds and the stocks of companies too small to meet the listing requirements for the national exchanges, as well as those of companies that prefer to have their stocks traded through many dealers rather than through the specialized dealers of the national exchanges.

Penny stocks. Stocks issued for the most part by companies with little experience, which therefore are more risky than stocks in proven corporations. So called because originally they could be purchased for less than one dollar.

Ponzi. One of the oldest and simplest forms of investment swindle, in which the victims' money is never invested in anything. Early investors are paid "gains" out of money put up by later investors, and the process continues until the bubble finally bursts. The scheme was named after Charles Ponzi of Boston, who lured victims into "investing" millions before the fraud was uncovered.

Portfolio. The list of securities held by an individual or institution, or the commercial paper held by a bank or other financial house.

Promoter. A person or firm that directly or indirectly takes the initiative in trying to induce individuals or organizations to put money into an enterprise or to purchase securities or other investments.

Prospectus. A publication, required by law, that describes each security being offered for sale to the public. A prospectus includes disclosures regarding risk, financial statements, management, and business purposes.

Pyramid scheme. A fraudulent scheme wherein an investor is sold the right to become a sales representative or member, often at a substantial price, thereby gaining the right to sell the same privilege to others. The sale of a "product" may be included in the scheme but is always secondary to the recruitment of new members. Those in the scheme early may profit; those in late always lose.

Receivership. A situation in which a receiver has been appointed by a court to take custody of, control, and manage the property or funds of another, pending judicial action concerning them.

Reparations award. The amount of monetary damages a party has been ordered by law to pay.

Respondent. The individual or firm against which a complaint has been filed and from which a reparations award or sanction is sought.

Risk capital. See *Venture capital.*

SEC. The Securities and Exchange Commission, established by Congress to regulate the securities industry and protect the investing public from fraud and mismanagement.

Security. Any note, stock, bond, investment contract, or similar instrument.

Service fee. A firm policy fee charged to a customer in lieu of commissions for services rendered.

Shell. A company or other organization without tangible assets or any valid business activity.

Spot market price. The price at which a physical commodity is selling at a given time and place.

Stripper well. A well that produces such a small volume of oil that the gross income from it produces only a small margin of profit.

Tax shelter. Investment plan that uses tax losses to offset or "shelter" the investor's taxable income from other sources. While some such plans are valid, others are illegal and subject to fines and penalties. (See *Abusive tax shelters.*)

Time-sharing. A plan in which individuals or groups can share in the ownership or rental of property that each will use only on a part-time basis.

Unauthorized trading. Purchase or sale of securities or other investments by a broker without the customer's permission.

Venture capital. Money invested in new, speculative firms or in new enterprises being developed by existing firms, in the hope that the venture will succeed and the returns on the investment will be substantial. Also known as "risk capital."

Warrant. A certificate giving the holder the right to purchase a security at a stipulated price, either perpetually or within a specified time. Warrants are sometimes included in a securities offering as inducements to buy.

Zero-coupon bonds. These bonds are so named because there are no (zero) semiannual interest coupon payments, as there are with other bonds. They can be purchased at a fraction of what will be their value at maturity, sometimes at just a few pennies on the dollar. They are sometimes used promotionally as "bonuses" to induce prospects to buy expensive items, a practice that can be misleading because they may not mature to face value for 25 years or more.

Appendix A

The Council of Better Business Bureaus is a business-supported nonprofit organization devoted to the protection of the consuming public and the vitality of the free enterprise system. Serving as the national headquarters for the local Better Business Bureaus, the Council promotes truth in advertising, resolves consumer/business disputes, develops industry standards for advertising and sales, and conducts consumer information programs.

COUNCIL OF BETTER BUSINESS BUREAUS, INC.
1515 Wilson Boulevard
Arlington, VA 22209
(703) 276-0100

Local Bureaus

ALABAMA
THE BBB, INC.
P.O. Box 55268
1214 S. 20th Street
Birmingham, AL 35205
(205) 933-2893

BBB OF NORTH ALABAMA, INC.
501 Church Street, NW
Huntsville, AL 35801
(205) 533-1640

BBB OF SOUTH ALABAMA, INC.
707 Van Antwerp Building
Mobile, AL 36602
(205) 433-5494, 95

The Better Business Bureau, Inc.
Union Bank Building
Commerce Street
Suite 810
Montgomery, AL 36104
(205) 262-5606

ALASKA
BBB OF ALASKA, INC.
3380 C Street, Suite 100
Anchorage, AK 99503
(907) 562-0704

ARIZONA
BBB OF MARICOPA COUNTY, INC.
4428 North 12th Street
Phoenix, AZ 85014
(602) 264-1721

BBB OF TUCSON, INC.
50 W. Drachman Street
Suite 103
Tucson, AZ 85705
(602) 622-7651

ARKANSAS
BBB OF ARKANSAS, INC.
1415 South University Avenue
Little Rock, AR 72204
(501) 664-7274

CALIFORNIA
BBB OF SOUTH CENTRAL
CALIFORNIA, INC.
705 Eighteenth Street
Bakersfield, CA 93301-4882
(805) 322-2074

BBB OF INLAND CITIES
290 N. 10th Street, Suite 206
P.O. Box 970
Colton, CA 92324-0522
(714) 825-7280

BBB OF CENTRAL
CALIFORNIA, INC.
5070 North Sixth, Suite 176
Fresno, CA 93710
(209) 222-8111

BBB OF MONTEREY, INC.
494 Alvarado Street
Monterey, CA 93940
(408) 372-3149

BBB, INC.
510 16th Street, Suite 550
Oakland, CA 94612
(415) 839-5900

SACRAMENTO VALLEY BBB
400 S Street
Sacramento, CA 95814
(916) 443-6843

BBB OF SAN DIEGO, LTD.
Union Bank Building, Suite 301
525 B Street
San Diego, CA 92101-4408
(619) 234-0966

BBB OF SAN FRANCISCO
33 New Montgomery St. Tower
San Francisco, CA 94105
(415) 243-9999

BBB OF SANTA CLARA
VALLEY, LTD.
1505 Meridian Avenue
San Jose, CA 95125
(408) 978-8700

BBB OF SAN MATEO
COUNTY, INC.
P.O. Box 294
20 North San Mateo Drive
San Mateo, CA 94401
(415) 347-1251

BBB OF TRI-COUNTIES
P.O. Box 746
111 No. Milpas Street
Santa Barbara, CA 93102
(805) 963-8657

BBB OF MID COUNTIES, INC.
1111 North Center Street
Stockton, CA 95202
(209) 948-4880, 81

COLORADO
BBB OF THE PIKES PEAK
REGION, INC.
3022 N. El Paso
Colorado Springs, CO 80907
(303) 636-1155

ROCKY MOUNTAIN BBB, INC.
1780 South Bellaire, Suite 700
Denver, CO 80222
(303) 758-8200

BBB OF NORTHERN
COLORADO, INC.
1730 South College Avenue
Suite 303
Fort Collins, CO 80525
(303) 484-1348

BBB OF SOUTHERN
COLORADO, INC.
432 Broadway & Grant
Pueblo, CO 81004
(303) 542-6464

CONNECTICUT
BBB OF WESTERN
CONNECTICUT, INC.
Fairfield Woods Plaza
P.O. Box 1410
2345 Black Rock Turnpike
Fairfield, CT 06430
(203) 374-6161

178

BBB OF NORTHERN
    CONNECTICUT, INC.
630 Oakwood Avenue
Suite 223
West Hartford, CT 06110
(203) 247-8700

BBB OF SE CONNECTICUT,
    INC.
100 S. Turnpike Road
Wallingford, CT 06492
(203) 269-2700, 269-4457

DELAWARE
KENT SUSSEX BBB, INC.
20 South Walnut Street
P.O. Box 300
Milford, DE 19963
(302) 422-6300 (Kent)
(302) 856-6969 (Sussex)

BBB OF DELAWARE, INC.
2055 Limestone Road,
Suite 200
P.O. Box 5361
Wilmington, DE 19808
(302) 996-9200

DISTRICT OF COLUMBIA
BBB OF METROPOLITAN
    WASHINGTON
1012 14th Street, NW
14th Floor
Washington, D.C. 20005
(202) 393-8000

FLORIDA
BBB OF WEST FLORIDA, INC.
13770 58th Street, N
Suite 309
Clearwater, FL 33520
(813) 535-5522
Sarasota & Manatee
(813) 957-0093

BBB OF SOUTH FLORIDA,
    INC.
Lee/Collier Division
3089 Cleveland Avenue
P.O. Box 2155
Fort Myers, FL 33902
(813) 334-7331, 7152

BBB OF NORTHEAST
    FLORIDA, INC.
3100 University Boulevard,
    South
Suite 239
Jacksonville, FL 32216
(904) 721-2288

BBB OF SOUTH FLORIDA,
    INC.
16291 Northwest 57th Avenue
Miami, FL 33014-6709
(305) 625-0307

BBB OF CENTRAL FLORIDA,
    INC.
132 E. Colonial Drive
Suite 213
Orlando, FL 32801
(305) 843-8873

BBB OF NORTHWEST
    FLORIDA, INC.
P.O. Box 1511
Pensacola, FL 32597-1511
(904) 433-6111

BBB OF PALM BEACH,
    MARTIN & ST. LUCIE
    COUNTIES
2247 Palm Beach Lakes Blvd.
Suite 211
West Palm Beach, FL 33409-
    3408
(407) 686-2200

GEORGIA
BBB OF METROPOLITAN
    ATLANTA, INC.
100 Edgewood Avenue
Suite 1012
Atlanta, GA 30303
(404) 688-4910

BBB OF AUGUSTA, INC.
624 Ellis Street
Suite 106
Augusta, GA 30901
(404) 722-1574

BBB OF WEST GEORGIA-
    EAST ALABAMA, INC.
Eight 13th Street
P.O. Box 2587
Columbus, GA 31902
(404) 324-0712, 13

BBB OF THE COASTAL
    EMPIRE, INC.
6822 Abercorn Street
P.O. Box 13956
Savannah, GA 31416-0956
(912) 354-7521

HAWAII
BBB OF HAWAII, INC.
1600 Kapiolani Blvd., Suite 714
Honolulu, HI 96814
(808) 942-2355

IDAHO
BBB OF TREASURE VALLEY, INC.
409 W. Jefferson
Boise, ID 83702
(208) 342-4649

BBB OF EASTERN IDAHO,
    INC.
545 Shoup - Suite 239
Idaho Falls, ID 83402
(208) 523-9754

ILLINOIS
BBB OF CHICAGO &
    NORTHERN ILLINOIS, INC.
211 West Wacker Drive
Chicago, IL 60601
(312) 444-1188

BBB OF CENTRAL ILLINOIS,
    INC.
109 S.W. Jefferson Street
Suite 305
Peoria, IL 61602
(309) 673-5194

INDIANA
BBB OF ELKHART COUNTY,
    INC.
118 South Second Street
P.O. Box 405
Elkhart, IN 46515
(219) 293-5731

EVANSVILLE REGIONAL BBB
119 S.E. Fourth Street
Evansville, IN 47708
(812) 422-6879

BBB OF NORTHEASTERN
    INDIANA, INC.
1203 Webster Street
Fort Wayne, IN 46802
(219) 423-4433

BBB OF NORTHWEST
    INDIANA, INC.
4231 Cleveland Street
Gary, IN 46408
(219) 980-1511

CENTRAL INDIANA BBB, INC.
Victoria Centre
22 E. Washington Street
Suite 310
Indianapolis, IN 46204
(317) 637-0197

BBB OF NORTHEASTERN
    INDIANA, INC.
204 Iroquois Building
Marion, IN 46952
(317) 668-8954, 55

BALL STATE UNIVERSITY
    BBB
Whitinger Building
Room 160
P.O. Box 192
Muncie, IN 47306
(317) 285-5668

179

BBB OF MICHIANA, INC.
50985 US #33, North
South Bend, IN 46637
(219) 277-9121

IOWA
BBB/QUAD CITIES
Alpine Centre
2435 Kimberly Road
Suite 110-N
Bettendorf, IA 52722
(319) 355-6344

CEDAR RAPIDS AREA BBB
1500 Second Avenue, S.E.
Suite 212
Cedar Rapids, IA 52403
(319) 366-5401

BBB OF CENTRAL &
EASTERN IOWA
615 Insurance Exchange
Building
Des Moines, IA 50309
(515) 243-8137

BBB OF SIOUXLAND, INC.
318 Badgerow Building
Sioux City, IA 51101
(712) 252-4501

KANSAS
BBB OF NORTHEAST
KANSAS, INC.
501 Jefferson - Suite 24
Topeka, KS 66607
(913) 232-0455

BBB INC.
300 Kaufman Building
Wichita, KS 67202
(316) 263-3146

KENTUCKY
BBB OF CENTRAL
KENTUCKY, INC.
154 Patchen Dr., Suite 90
Lexington, KY 40502
(606) 268-4128

THE BBB, INC.
844 South 4th Street
Louisville, KY 40203
(502) 583-6546

LOUISIANA
BBB ALEXANDRIA-PINEVILLE
1407 Murray Street
Suite 101
Alexandria, LA 71301
(318) 473-4494

BBB OF SOUTH CENTRAL
LA, INC.
2055 Wooddale Blvd.
Baton Rouge, LA 70806
(504) 926-3010

BBB - TRI PARISH AREA
300 Bond Street
Houma, LA 70361
(504) 868-3456

BBB OF ACADIANA, INC.
100 Huggins Road
P.O. Box 30297
Lafayette, LA 70593
(318) 981-3497

BBB OF SOUTHWEST
LOUISIANA, INC.
1413-C Ryan Street
P.O. Box 1681
Lake Charles, LA 70602
(318) 433-1633

BBB OF NORTHEAST
LOUISIANA, INC.
141 De Siard Street - Suite 300
Monroe, LA 71201
(318) 387-4600, 01

BBB OF GREATER NEW
ORLEANS AREA, INC.
1539 Jackson Ave., Suite 400
New Orleans, LA 70130
(504) 581-6222

THE BBB
1401 North Market Street
Shreveport, LA 71107
(318) 221-8352

MAINE
BBB OF MAINE, INC.
812 Stevens Avenue
Portland, ME 04103
(207) 878-2715

MARYLAND
BBB OF GREATER
MARYLAND, INC.
401 North Howard Street
Baltimore, MD 21201
(301) 347-3990

MASSACHUSETTS
THE BBB, INC.
8 Winter Street - 6th Floor
Boston, MA 02108
(617) 482-9151

BBB OF METRO WEST
One Kendall Street
Suite 307
Framingham, MA 01701
(617) 872-5585

BBB OF CAPE COD & THE
ISLANDS
78 North Street - Suite 1
Hyannis, MA 02501
(617) 771-3022

BBB OF MERRIMACK VALLEY
316 Essex Street
Lawrence, MA 01840
(617) 687-7666

BBB OF SE MASSACHUSETTS,
INC.
106 State Road - Suite 4
North Dartmouth, MA 02747
(617) 999-6060

BBB OF WESTERN
MASSACHUSETTS, INC.
293 Bridge Street - Suite 324
Springfield, MA 01103
(413) 734-3114

BBB OF CENTRAL NEW
ENGLAND, INC.
32 Franklin Street
P.O. Box 379
Worcester, MA 01601
(617) 755-2548

MICHIGAN
BBB OF DETROIT & E.
MICHIGAN, INC.
150 Michigan Avenue
Detroit, MI 48226-2646
(313) 962-7566

BBB OF WESTERN
MICHIGAN, INC.
620 Trust Building
Grand Rapids, MI 49503
(616) 774-8236

MINNESOTA
BBB OF MINNESOTA
1745 University Avenue
St. Paul, MN 55104
(612) 646-4631

MISSISSIPPI
BBB OF MISSISSIPPI/Biloxi
Branch
2917 W. Beach Blvd.
Suite 103
Biloxi, MS 39531
(601) 374-2222

BBB OF MISSISSIPPI/
Columbus Branch
105 Fifth Street
Columbus, MS 39701
(601) 327-8594

BBB OF MISSISSIPPI, INC.
510 George Street - Suite 107
P.O. Box 2090
Jackson, MS 39225-2090
(601) 948-8222

BBB OF MISSISSIPPI/Meridian
Branch
P.O. Box 5512
Meridian, MS 39302
(601) 482-8752

MISSOURI
BBB OF GREATER KANSAS
CITY, INC.
306 East 12th Street
Suite 1024
Kansas City, MO 64106
(816) 421-7800

BBB OF E. MISSOURI & SO.
ILLINOIS
5100 Oakland, Suite 200
St. Louis, MO 63110
(314) 531-3300

BBB OF SOUTHWEST
MISSOURI, INC.
205 Park Central East,
Suite 509
P.O. Box 4331 GS
Springfield, MO 65806
(417) 862-9231

NEBRASKA
CORNHUSKER BBB, INC.
719 North 48th Street
Lincoln, NE 68504
(402) 467-5261

BBB OF OMAHA, INC.
1613 Farnam Street,
Room 417
Omaha, NE 68102
(402) 346-3033

NEVADA
BBB OF SOUTHERN NEVADA,
INC.
1022 E. Sahara Avenue
Las Vegas, NV 89104
(702) 735-6900

BBB OF NORTHERN NEVADA,
INC.
991 Bible Way
P.O. Box 21269
Reno, NV 89515
(702) 322-0657

NEW HAMPSHIRE
BBB OF GRANITE STATE
410 Main Street
Concord, NH 03301
(603) 224-1991

NEW JERSEY
BBB OF GREATER NEWARK,
INC.
34 Park Place
Newark, NJ 07102
(201) 643-3025

BBB OF BERGEN, PASSAIC &
ROCKLAND COUNTIES
2 Forest Avenue
Paramus, NJ 07652
(201) 845-4044

OCEAN COUNTY BBB
1721 Route 37 East
Toms River, NJ 08753
(201) 270-5577

BBB OF CENTRAL NEW
JERSEY, INC.
1700 Whitehorse
Hamilton Square, Suite D-5
Trenton, NJ 08690
Mercer County
(609) 588-0808
Monmouth County
(201) 536-6306
Middlesex, Somerset &
Hunderton Counties
(201) 329-6855

BBB OF SOUTH JERSEY, INC.
16 Maple Avenue
P.O. Box 303
Westmont, NJ 08108-0303
(609) 854-8467

NEW MEXICO
BBB OF NEW MEXICO, INC.
4600-A Montgomery, N.E.
Suite 200
Albuquerque, NM 87109
(505) 884-0500

BBB/FOUR CORNERS, INC.
308 North Locke
Farmington, NM 87401
(505) 326-6501

BBB OF SANTA FE
1210 Luisa Street
Suite 5
Santa Fe, NM 87502
(505) 988-3648

NEW YORK
BBB OF WESTERN NEW
YORK, INC.
775 Main Street
Suite 401
Buffalo, NY 14203
(716) 856-7180

LONG ISLAND BBB
266 Main Street
Farmingdale, NY 11735
(516) 420-0500

BBB OF METROPOLITAN
NEW YORK, INC.
257 Park Avenue South
New York, NY 10010
(212) 533-6200

BBB OF ROCHESTER, INC.
1122 Sibley Tower
Rochester, NY 14604
(716) 546-6776

BBB, INC. SERVING CENTRAL
NY, THE NORTH COUNTRY
& THE SOUTHERN TIER
100 University Building
Syracuse, NY 13202
(315) 479-6635

BBB OF WESTCHESTER,
PUTNAM AND DUCHESS
COUNTIES
One Brockway Place
White Plains, NY 10601
(914) 428-1230, 31
120 E. Main Street
Wappingers Falls, NY 12590
(914) 297-6550

NORTH CAROLINA
THE BBB OF ASHEVILLE/
WESTERN NORTH
CAROLINA, INC.
29 1/2 Page Avenue
Asheville, NC 28801
(704) 253-2392

THE BBB OF THE SOUTHERN
PIEDMONT, INC.
1130 East 3rd Street
Suite 400
Charlotte, NC 28204
(704) 332-7151

BBB OF CENTRAL NORTH
CAROLINA, INC.
3608 West Friendly Avenue
Greensboro, NC 27410
(919) 852-4240, 41, 42

BBB OF CATAWBA COUNTY
P.O. Box 1882
Hickory, NC 28603
(704) 464-0372

BBB OF EASTERN NORTH
CAROLINA, INC.
3120 Poplarwood Drive
Suite G-1
Raleigh, NC 27604
(919) 872-9240

THE BBB, INC.
2110 Cloverdale Avenue
Suite 2-B
Winston-Salem, NC 27103
(919) 725-8348

OHIO
BBB OF AKRON, INC.
137 South Main Street
Suite 200
P.O. Box 596
Akron, OH 44308
(216) 253-4590

BBB OF STARK COUNTY,
INC.
1434 Cleveland Avenue, NW
Canton, OH 44703
(216) 454-9401

CINCINNATI BBB, INC.
898 Walnut Street
Cincinnati, OH 45202
(513) 421-3015

THE BBB, INC.
2217 East 9th Street
Cleveland, OH 44115
(216) 241-7678

BBB OF CENTRAL OHIO, INC.
527 South High Street
Columbus, OH 43215
(614) 221-6336

BBB OF DAYTON/MIAMI
VALLEY, INC.
40 West Fourth Street
Suite 280
Dayton, OH 45402
(513) 222-5825

MANSFIELD AREA BBB
130 W. 2nd Street
P.O. Box 1706
Mansfield, OH 44901
(419) 522-1700

BBB SERVING NW OHIO &
SE MICHIGAN, INC.
425 Jefferson Avenue
Suite 909
Toledo, OH 43604-1055
(419) 241-6276

WOOSTER AREA BBB
345 N. Market
Wooster, OH 44691
(216) 263-6444

BBB OF MAHONING VALLEY,
INC.
311 Mahoning Bank Building
P.O. Box 1495
Youngstown, OH 44501
(216) 744-3111

OKLAHOMA
BBB OF CENTRAL
OKLAHOMA, INC.
17 S. Dewey
Oklahoma City, OK 73102
(405) 239-6084

BBB OF TULSA, INC.
4833 South Sheridan
Suite 412
Tulsa, OK 74145
(918) 664-1266

OREGON
PORTLAND BBB, INC.
520 SW Sixth Avenue
Suite 600
Portland, OR 97204
(503) 226-3981

PENNSYLVANIA
LEHIGH VALLEY BBB OF
EASTERN PA
528 North New Street
Bethlehem, PA 18018
(215) 866-8780

CAPITAL DIVISION OF BBB
OF EASTERN PA
53 North Duke Street
Lancaster, PA 17602
(717) 291-1151

BBB OF EASTERN
PENNSYLVANIA
1930 Chestnut Street
P.O. Box 2297
Philadelphia, PA 19103
(215) 496-1000

BBB OF WESTERN
PENNSYLVANIA, INC.
610 Smithfield Street
Pittsburgh, PA 15222
(412) 456-2700

BBB OF NORTHEASTERN PA,
INC.
601 Connell Building
6th floor
P.O. Box 993
Scranton, PA 18501
(717) 342-9129

PUERTO RICO
BBB OF PUERTO RICO, INC.
GPO Box 70212
San Juan, PR 00936
(809) 756-5400

RHODE ISLAND
BBB OF RHODE ISLAND, INC.
100 Bignall Street
Bureau Park—Box 1300
Warwick, RI 02887-1300
(401) 785-1212

SOUTH CAROLINA
BBB OF THE MIDLANDS
1830 Bull Street
Columbia, SC 29201
(803) 254-2525

BBB OF THE FOOTHILLS
311 Pettigru Street
Greenville, SC 29601
(803) 242-5052

BBB OF COASTAL
CAROLINA, INC.
831 Flatiron Bldg., Suite 12
Highway #17, North
Myrtle Beach, SC 29577
(803) 448-6100

TENNESSEE
BBB, INC.
Park Plaza Building
1010 Market Street
Suite 200
Chattanooga, TN 37402
(615) 266-6144

BBB OF GREATER EAST
TENNESSEE, INC.
900 East Hill Avenue,
Suite 165
P.O. Box 10327
Knoxville, TN 37939-0327
(615) 522-1300

MEMPHIS AREA BBB, INC.
1835 Union - Suite 312
P.O. Box 41406
Memphis, TN 38174-1406
(901) 272-9641

BBB OF NASHVILLE/MIDDLE
TENNESSEE, INC.
506 Nashville City Bank Bldg.
Nashville, TN 37201
(615) 254-5872

TEXAS
BBB OF ABILENE, INC.
Bank of Commerce Bldg.
Suite 320
P.O. Box 3275
Abilene, TX 79604
(915) 691-1533

BBB OF THE GOLDEN
SPREAD
6900 I-40 West
Suite 275
Amarillo, TX 79106
(806) 374-3735

THE BBB, INC.
1005 MBank Plaza
Austin, TX 78701
(512) 476-6943

BBB OF SOUTHEAST TEXAS,
INC.
476 Oakland Avenue
P.O. Box 2988
Beaumont, TX 77704
(409) 835-5348

BBB OF BRAZOS VALLEY,
INC.
202 Varisco Building
Bryan, TX 77803
(409) 823-8148, 49

BBB OF THE COASTAL
BEND, INC.
109 N. Chaparral - Suite 101
Corpus Christi, TX 78401
(512) 888-5555

BBB OF METRO DALLAS,
INC.
2001 Bryan Street - Suite 850
Dallas, TX 75201
(214) 220-2000

BBB OF PASO DEL NORTE,
INC.
Better Business Building
1910 East Yandell
El Paso, TX 79903
(915) 545-1212

BBB AT FORT WORTH
SERVING TARRANT,
JOHNSON, HOOD,
WISE, PARKER & PALO
PINTO COUNTIES, INC.
709 Sinclair Building
106 West 5th Street
Fort Worth, TX 76102
(817) 332-7585

BBB OF METROPOLITAN
HOUSTON, INC.
2707 North Loop West
Suite 900
Houston, TX 77008
(713) 868-9500

BBB OF THE SOUTH PLAINS,
INC.
1015 15th Street
P.O. Box 1178
Lubbock, TX 79408
(806) 763-0459

BBB OF THE PERMIAN
BASIN, INC.
Airport Road 20
P.O. Box 6006
Midland, TX 79711
(915) 563-1880

BBB OF SAN ANGELO, INC.
1207 S. Bryant
P.O. Box 3366
San Angelo, TX 76902-3366
(915) 653-2318

THE BETTER BUSINESS
BUREAU
1800 Northeast Loop 410
Suite 400
San Antonio, TX 78217
(512) 828-9441

BBB OF CENTRAL EAST
TEXAS, INC.
3502-D South Broadway
P.O. Box 6652
Tyler, TX 75711-6652
(214) 581-5704

BBB OF WACO, INC.
6801 Sanger Avenue
Suite 125
P.O. Box 7203
Waco, TX 76714-7203
(817) 772-7530

BBB OF SOUTH TEXAS, INC.
P.O. Box 69
Weslaco, TX 78596-0069
(512) 968-3678

BBB OF NORTH CENTRAL
TEXAS, INC.
1106 Brook Street
Wichita Falls, TX 76301-5009
(817) 723-5526

UTAH
THE BBB, INC.
385 - 24th Street - Suite 717
Ogden, UT 84401
(801) 399-4701

BBB OF UTAH
1588 South Main Street
Salt Lake City, UT 84115
(801) 487-4656

VIRGINIA
BBB OF GREATER HAMPTON
ROADS, INC.
3608 Tidewater Drive
Norfolk, VA 23509
(804) 627-5651

BBB OF CENTRAL VIRGINIA,
INC.
701 East Franklin - Suite 712
Richmond, VA 23219
(804) 648-0016

BBB OF WESTERN VIRGINIA,
INC.
121 West Campbell Avenue
Roanoke, VA 24011-1290
(703) 342-3455

WASHINGTON
TRI-CITY BBB, INC.
127 W. Canal Drive
Kennewick, WA 99336
(509) 582-0222

BETTER BUSINESS BUREAU
2401 Bristol Court
Olympia, WA 98502
(206) 754-4254

BBB OF GREATER SEATTLE,
INC.
828 Denny Building
2200 Sixth Avenue
Seattle, WA 98121
(206) 448-8888

BBB OF THE INLAND
NORTHWEST
South 176 Stevens
Spokane, WA 99204
(509) 747-1155

THE BBB, INC.
1101 Fawcett Avenue #222
P.O. Box 1274
Tacoma, WA 98401
(206) 383-5561

BBB OF CENTRAL
WASHINGTON, INC.
418 Washington Mutual
Building
P.O. Box 1584
Yakima, WA 98907
(509) 248-1326

WISCONSIN
BBB OF GREATER
MILWAUKEE
740 North Plankinton Avenue
Milwaukee, WI 53203
(414) 273-1600

Appendix B

The North American Securities Administrators Association is an organization comprised of all state and provincial securities administrators in the United States and Canada who are charged with enforcing their jurisdictions' securities laws and protecting the public from fraudulent investments.

NORTH AMERICAN SECURITIES ADMINISTRATORS ASSOCIATION, INC.
555 New Jersey Avenue, N.W.
Suite 750
Washington, DC 20001
(202) 737-0900

ALABAMA
Securities Commission
166 Commerce Street, 2nd
Floor
Montgomery, AL 36130
(205) 261-2984

ALASKA
Department of Commerce &
Economic Development
Division of Banking,
Securities, and
Corporations
State Office Building
333 Willoughby, 9th Floor
P.O. Box D
Juneau, AK 99811-0800
(907) 465-2521

ALBERTA
Securities Commission
10025 Jasper Avenue, 21st
Floor
Edmonton, Alberta
T5J 3Z5 Canada
(403) 427-5201

ARIZONA
Corporation Commission
Securities Division
1200 West Washington
Phoenix, AZ 85007
(602) 255-4242

ARKANSAS
Securities Department
Heritage West Building
201 East Markham, 3rd Floor
Little Rock, AR 72201
(501) 371-1011

BRITISH COLUMBIA
Securities Commission
865 Hornby Street, 11th Floor
Vancouver, British Columbia
V6Z 2H4 Canada
(604) 660-4800

CALIFORNIA
Department of Corporations
600 South Commonwealth
Avenue
Los Angeles, CA 90005
(213) 736-2741

COLORADO
Division of Securities
1560 Broadway, Suite 1450
Denver, CO 80202
(303) 894-2320

CONNECTICUT
Department of Banking
Securities and Business
Investments Division
State of Connecticut
44 Capitol Avenue
Hartford, CT 06106
(203) 566-4560

DELAWARE
Division of Securities
Department of Justice
State Office Building
820 N. French Street, 8th
Floor
Wilmington, DE 19801
(302) 571-2515

DISTRICT OF COLUMBIA
Public Service Commission
Division of Securities
450 5th Street, N.W.
Suite 820
Washington, DC 20001
(202) 626-5105

FLORIDA
Office of Comptroller
Department of Banking and
Finance
Division of Securities
The Capitol
Tallahassee, FL 32301-8054
(904) 488-9805

GEORGIA
Division of Business Services
and Regulations
Secretary of State
2 Martin Luther King, Jr.
Drive
Suite 315, West Tower
Atlanta, GA 30334
(404) 656-2894

HAWAII
Department of Commerce
and Consumer Affairs
1010 Richards Street
P.O. Box 40
Honolulu, HI 96810
(808) 548-6521

IDAHO
Department of Finance
Statehouse
700 West State Street
Boise, ID 83720
(208) 334-3684

ILLINOIS
Office of the Secretary of
State
Securities Department
900 South Spring Street
Springfield, IL 62704
(217) 782-2256

Office of the Director
188 West Randolph Street,
Room 426
Chicago, IL 60601
(312) 793-3384

INDIANA
Office of the Secretary of
State
Securities Division
One North Capitol, Suite 560
Indianapolis, IN 46204
(317) 232-6681

IOWA
Insurance Department of
  Iowa
Securities Division
Lucas State Office Building
Des Moines, IA 50319
(515) 281-4441

KANSAS
Securities Commissioner
Landon State Office Building
900 S.W. Jackson Street,
Suite 552
Topeka, KS 66612-1220
(913) 296-3307

KENTUCKY
Department of Banking and
  Securities
Division of Securities
911 Leawood Drive
Frankfort, KY 40601
(502) 564-2180

LOUISIANA
Securities Commission
315 Louisiana State Office
  Building
325 Loyola Avenue
New Orleans, LA 70112
(504) 568-5515

MAINE
Department of Professional
  and Financial Regulation
Bureau of Banking
Securities Division
State House Station 121
Augusta, ME 04333
(207) 582-8760

MANITOBA
Securities Commission
1128-405 Broadway Avenue
Winnipeg, Manitoba
R3C 3L6 Canada
(204) 945-2548

MARYLAND
State Law Department
Division of Securities
Munsey Building
7 North Calvert Street
Baltimore, MD 21202
(301) 576-6360

MASSACHUSETTS
Secretary of the
  Commonwealth
Securities Division
John W. McCormack Building
One Ashburton Place, Rm.1719
Boston, MA 02108
(617) 727-3548

MEXICO
Comision Nacional de
  Valores
Barranca del Muerto No. 275
Col. San Jose Insurgentes
Mexico 03900, D.F.
(905) 593-9855

MICHIGAN
Department of Commerce
Corporation & Securities
  Bureau
6546 Mercantile Way
P.O. Box 30222
Lansing, MI 48909
(517) 334-6206

MINNESOTA
Department of Commerce
500 Metro Square Building
St. Paul, MN 55101
(612) 296-6848

MISSISSIPPI
Office of the Secretary of
  State
Securities Division
P.O. Box 136
401 Mississippi Street
Jackson, MS 39205
(601) 359-1350

MISSOURI
Office of the Secretary of
  State
Commissioner of Securities
Truman State Office Building
Jefferson City, MO 65102
(314) 751-4136

MONTANA
Office of the State Auditor
Securities Department
Mitchell Building, Room 270
126 N. Sanders
P.O. Box 4009
Helena, MT 59604
(406) 444-2040

NEBRASKA
Department of Banking &
  Finance
Bureau of Securities
301 Centennial Mall South
P.O. Box 95006
Lincoln, NE 68509
(402) 471-3445

NEVADA
Department of State
Securities Division
2501 E. Sahara Avenue
Las Vegas, NV 89158
(702) 486-4400
Carson City Office
(702) 885-5203

NEW BRUNSWICK
Securities Act
Provincial Building
110 Charlotte Street
P.O. Box 5001
Saint John, New Brunswick
E2L 4Y9 Canada
(506) 658-2504

NEWFOUNDLAND
Department of Justice
Registry of Deeds, Companies
  and Securities
Confederation Building
P.O. Box 4750
St. Johns, Newfoundland
A1C 5T7 Canada
(709) 576-3316

NEW HAMPSHIRE
Office of Securities
  Regulation
157 Manchester Street
Concord, NH 03301
(603) 271-1463

NEW JERSEY
Department of Law & Public
  Safety
Bureau of Securities
Two Gateway Center, 8th
  Floor
Newark, NJ 07102
(201) 648-2040

NEW MEXICO
Regulation and Licensing
  Department
Securities Division
Bataan Memorial Building,
  Room 165
Santa Fe, NM 87503
(505) 827-7750

NEW YORK
Department of Law
Bureau of Investor Protection
and Securities
120 Broadway - 23rd Floor
New York, NY 10271
(212) 341-2222

NORTH CAROLINA
Department of State
Securities Division
300 North Salisbury Street,
Room 404
Raleigh, NC 27611
(919) 733-3924

NORTH DAKOTA
Securities Commissioner
State Capitol
Bismarck, ND 58505
(701) 224-2910

**NORTHWEST
TERRITORIES**
Registrar of Securities
Government of the Northwest
Territories
Yellowknife, Northwest
Territories
X1A 2L9 Canada
(403) 873-7490

NOVA SCOTIA
Department of Attorney
General
Office of the Registrar
Under the Securities Act
Joseph Howe Bldg., 2nd Floor
1690 Hollis Street
P.O. Box 458
Halifax, Nova Scotia
B3J 3J9 Canada
(902) 424-7768

OHIO
Department of Commerce
Division of Securities
Two Nationwide Plaza
Columbus, OH 43266-0548
(614) 644-7381

OKLAHOMA
Securities Commission
Will Rogers Memorial Office
Bldg.
2401 Lincoln Blvd., 4th Floor
P.O. Box 53595
Oklahoma City, OK 73152
(405) 521-2451

ONTARIO
Ontario Securities
Commission
P.O. Box 55
20 Queen Street West,
Suite 1800
Toronto, Ontario
M5H 3S8 Canada
(416) 593-8200

OREGON
Department of Insurance and
Finance
Division of Finance and
Corporate Securities
21 Labor and Industries Bldg.
Salem, OR 97310
(503) 378-4387

PENNSYLVANIA
Securities Commission
Eastgate Office Building,
2nd Floor
1010 North Seventh St.
Harrisburg, PA 17102-1410
(717) 787-8061

PRINCE EDWARD ISLAND
Department of Justice
Securities Act
Box 2000
Charlottetown,
Prince Edward Island
C1A 7N8 Canada
(902) 368-4550

PUERTO RICO
Office of the Commissioner
of Financial Institutions
Securities Office
GPO Call Box 70324
San Juan, PR 00936
Government Employees
Retirement Fund Building
437 Ponce de Leon Avenue,
14th Floor
Hato Rey, PR 00918
(809) 751-5606 or
(809) 751-7837

QUEBEC
Commission des valeurs
mobilières du Québec
P.O. Box 246
Stock Exchange Tower
Montréal, Québec
H4Z 1G3 Canada
(514) 873-5326

RHODE ISLAND
Department of Business
Regulation
Securities Division
233 Richmond St., Suite 232
Providence, RI 02903-4232
(401) 277-3048

SASKATCHEWAN
Securities Commission
T.D. Bank Building, 8th Floor
1914 Hamilton Street
Regina, Saskatchewan
S4P 3V7 Canada
(306) 787-5630

SOUTH CAROLINA
Department of State
Securities Division
Edgar Brown Building
1205 Pendleton Street, #501
Columbia, SC 29201
(803) 734-1087

SOUTH DAKOTA
Division of Securities
910 East Sioux Avenue
Pierre, SD 57501
(605) 773-4823

TENNESSEE
Department of Commerce
and Insurance
Securities Division
Doctors Building
706 Church Street, Suite 202
Nashville, TN 37219
(615) 741-2947

TEXAS
State Securities Board
P.O. Box 13167
Capitol Station
Austin, TX 78711-3167
(512) 474-2233

UTAH
Department of Business
Regulation
Securities Division
160 East 300 South or
P.O. Box 45802
Salt Lake City, UT 84145-0801
(801) 530-6600

VERMONT
Department of Banking &
Insurance
Securities Division
120 State Street
Montpelier, VT 05602
(802) 828-3301

VIRGINIA
Division of Securities and
Retail Franchising
State Corporation
Commission
P.O. Box 1197
Richmond, VA 23209
(804) 786-7751

WASHINGTON
Department of Licensing
  Business & Professions
  Administration
Securities Division
P.O. Box 648
Olympia, WA 98504
(206) 753-6928

WEST VIRGINIA
Securities Division
State Auditor's Office
State Capitol Building
Charleston, WV 25305
(304) 348-2257

WISCONSIN
Office of the Commissioner
  of Securities
111 West Wilson Street
P.O. Box 1768
Madison, WI 53701
(608) 266-3431

WYOMING
Secretary of State
Securities Division
State Capitol Building
Cheyenne, WY 82002
(307) 777-7370

YUKON TERRITORY
Government of Yukon
Consumer & Corporate
  Affairs
P.O. Box 2703
Whitehorse, Yukon Territory
Y1A 2C6 Canada
(403) 667-5225

Appendix C

The following list provides addresses and phone numbers for agencies and organizations referred to in this publication. The second column provides a sketch of the areas of activity of each organization as it relates to our topic.

The names, addresses, phone numbers, and office descriptions presented here have been thoroughly checked. However, because of changes that may take place after publication, some information may no longer be current. We regret any inconvenience this may cause.

These agencies and organizations	may provide answers and assistance in these areas
American Gemological Laboratories Gemline Recovery Service 580 Fifth Avenue New York, NY 10036 (212) 704-0727	questions involving possible fraud or misrepresentation in gem dealings
American Gem Society 5901 West 3rd Street Los Angeles, CA 90036-2898 (213) 936-4367	verifying membership of gem dealers; list of dealers in your area; guidelines for buying gems and jewelry
American Institute of Certified Public Accountants 1211 Avenue of the Americas New York, NY 10036 (212) 575-6200	confirming qualifications of CPAs
Commodity Futures Trading Commission (CFTC) 2033 K Street, N.W. Washington, DC 20581 (202) 254-8630	information regarding commodity futures trading; verifying licensing and complaint history of commodities firms

Regional CFTC Offices

Chicago
233 South Wacker Drive
Suite 4600
Chicago, IL 60606
(312) 886-9000

Kansas City
4901 Main Street
Room 400
Kansas City, MO 64112
(816) 374-2131

Los Angeles
10850 Wilshire Boulevard
Suite 370
Los Angeles, CA 90024
(213) 209-6782

Minneapolis
510 Grain Exchange
  Building
Minneapolis, MN 55415
(612) 370-3255

New York
One World Trade Center
Suite 4747
New York, NY 10048
(212) 466-5723

Direct Selling Association 1776 K Street, N.W. Suite 600 Washington, DC 20006 (202) 293-5760	verifying membership of companies involved in direct sales
Federal Trade Commission (FTC) 6th Street & Pennsylvania Ave., N.W. Washington, DC 20580 (202) 326-3128	questions involving deceptive business practices

Regional FTC Offices

Atlanta
1718 Peachtree Street, N.W.
Suite 1000
Atlanta, GA 30367
(404) 347-4836

Boston
10 Causeway Street
Room 1184
Boston, MA 02222-1073
(617) 565-7240

Chicago
55 East Monroe Street
Suite 1437
Chicago, IL 60603
(312) 353-4423

188

Cleveland
118 St. Clair Avenue
Suite 500
The Mall Building
Cleveland, OH 44114
(216) 522-4207
Dallas
8303 Elmbrook Drive
Suite 140
Dallas, TX 75247
(214) 767-7053

Denver
1405 Curtis Street
Suite 2900
Denver, CO 80202
(303) 844-2271
Los Angeles
11000 Wilshire Boulevard
Los Angeles, CA 90024
(213) 209-7575
New York
26 Federal Plaza
22nd Floor
New York, NY 10278
(212) 264-1207

San Francisco
901 Market Street
Suite 570
San Francisco, CA 94103
(415) 995-5220
Seattle
915 Second Avenue
Federal Building
Room 2806
Seattle, WA 98174
(206) 442-4655/56

Housing and Urban Development Department Interstate Land Sales Registration HUD Building 451 7th Street, S.W., Room 6262 Washington, DC 20410-8000 (202) 755-0502	verifying land sales registration; information regarding complaint history
Institute of Certified Financial Planners Two Denver Highlands 10065 East Harvard Avenue Suite 320 Denver, CO 80231 (303) 751-7600	information on how to select a financial planner; list of Certified Financial Planners in your area
International Association for Financial Planning 5775 Peachtree-Dunwoody Road Suite 120-C Atlanta, GA 30342 (404) 395-1605	verifying membership of financial planners; list of financial planners in your area
International Foundation for Art Research 46 East 70th Street New York, NY 10021 (212) 879-1780	general guidelines for purchasing art; authentication services
National Association of Home Builders 15th & M Streets, N.W. Washington, DC 20005 (202) 822-0200	general guidelines for buying a home; information on your local home builders association
National Association of Personal Financial Advisors 1130 Lake Cook Road Suite 105 Buffalo Grove, IL 60089 (312) 537-7722	verifying membership of financial advisors; list of financial advisors in your area
National Association of Securities Dealers 1735 K Street, N.W. Washington, DC 20006 (202) 728-8000	verifying membership of securities dealers; assistance with complaints
National Futures Association 200 West Madison Street Suite 1600 Chicago, IL 60606 (800) 572-9400—Illinois residents (800) 621-3570—outside Illinois	verifying registration of commodities firms/dealers; information regarding any NFA disciplinary actions, assistance in arbitrating claims; questions involving investors' rights

189

Professional Coin Grading Service
P.O. Box 9458
Newport Beach, CA 92658
(714) 250-1211

list of authorized dealers

Securities and Exchange Commission
(SEC)
450 Fifth Street, N.W.
Washington, DC 20006
(202) 272-7440

information on public stock
issues and securities fraud;
verifying registration of
securities brokers and
investment advisers

Regional SEC Offices

Atlanta
Suite 788
1375 Peachtree Street, N.E.
Atlanta, GA 30367
(404) 347-4768

Boston
J.W. McCormick Post Office &
Court House Building
Suite 700
Boston, MA 02109
(617) 223-9900

Chicago
Room 1204
Everett McKinley Dirksen Bldg.
219 South Dearborn Street
Chicago, IL 60604
(312) 353-7390

Denver
Suite 700
410 Seventeenth Street
Denver, CO 80202
(303) 844-2071

Fort Worth
8th Floor
411 West Seventh Street
Fort Worth, TX 76102
(817) 334-3821

Los Angeles
5757 Wilshire Boulevard
Suite 500 East
Los Angeles, CA 90036-
3648
(213) 468-3107

New York
Room 1102
26 Federal Plaza
New York, NY 10278
(212) 264-1636

Seattle
3040 Jackson Federal
Building
915 Second Avenue
Seattle, WA 98174
(206) 442-7990

Washington
Public Reference Branch
450 5th Street, N.W.
Washington, DC 20549
(202) 272-7450

Securities Investor Protection
Corporation
805 15th Street, N.W.
Washington, DC 20005-2207
(202) 371-8300

verifying membership of
brokers/dealers

United States Bureau of Land
Management
C & 19th Streets, N.W.
Washington, DC 20240
(202) 343-9435

information regarding land
auctions; oil and gas leasing

United States Postal Service
Chief Postal Inspector
Room 3509
Washington, DC 20260
(202) 268-4267

reporting phony invoices or
other fraud involving
documents sent through the
U.S. mail

Index

Abrams, Robert, 150
Account executive. *See* Stockbroker
Alabama Securities Commission (ASC), 83, 87, 133–34
Alderdice, James and William, 8–9, 11, 58
American College, 48
American Gemological Laboratories, 63, 66
American Gem Society, 66
American Institute of Certified Public Accountants, 166
Amsterdam Stock Exchange, 146
Arbitration, 165
Art prints, 148–52
Attorney General, 79, 117
  Consumer Fraud Division, 66
  New York, 24
Baum, Martin, 20–21
Beesley, C. R. ("Cap"), 63–65
Benny, Jack, 82
Bergen, Candice, 82
Berger, Andrew, 34–35
Berger, Lisa, 49
Better Business Bureau(s), 11, 133, 138, 168
  contacting for information, 14, 79, 113, 117, 155, 166
Bevill, Bresler & Schulman, 135
"Blind pool" offerings, 97
Boiler rooms, 64, 86–87, 98, 101–2, 142–55
Bonds, 43, 132–39
BPM, Ltd., 89
Brailsford, Kenneth, 100
Brotman, Stanley, 74
Bucket shops, 144, 146
Bullion, gold, 58, 59, 60, 66
Bureau of Securities of the State of New Jersey, 94
Business opportunity swindles, 21. *See also* Franchises
Buying "on margin," 162
"Cash forward" contracts, 38
Certificates of Accrual on Treasury Securities (CATs), 138
"Certified Financial Planner" (CFP), 48
Challenge, Inc., 171
"Churning," 36, 159, 164
Coins, 57, 58–59, 60, 66
College for Financial Planning, 47, 48
Commissions, 155
  for brokers and dealers, 37, 39, 61, 159, 161
  for financial planners, 43, 49
Commodities and futures, 13, 30–39, 106–8, 162
Commodity Exchange Act, 36
Commodity Futures Trading Commission (CFTC), 38, 165
Coral Island Club, 124
Council of Better Business Bureaus (CBBB), 12, 13, 37–38, 115, 116, 170
Counterfeiting, 66, 149–51
"Coupon treasury receipts," 133
"Culture Farms," 170
"Deferred" or "delayed" delivery, 9, 12, 38, 61, 66, 113
Department of Housing and Urban Development, 73
Derby-Vision, 153
Direct Selling Association, 117
Disclosure statement, 23–24, 38
"Distributorships." *See* Franchises
District attorney, 117
Drysdale Government Securities, 148

Dun & Bradstreet, 113
Eichler, Lawrence B., 46
Empire Savings & Loan Bank, 71–72
Escrow account, 79, 129, 155
Fabulous Fakes, 20
Face value (of bonds), 132–33, 139
Falcon Sciences, 85–86
FBI, 87
Federal Housing Authority, 73
Federal property report, 78
Federal Trade Commission (FTC), 23, 64
Federman, David, 64
Financial planner(s) and planning, 43–53
Financial statement, 14, 24–25, 39
First Commodity Corporation, 36
First National City Bank, 82
"Fixed maturity" contracts, 38
Forgery, art print, 149–51
Fractional interests (oil and gas), 87, 91
Franchises, 18–27
Fraud statutes, 64
Freedom Coin Company, 100
FSLIC, 71
Futures. *See* Commodities and futures
Gemline Recovery Service (GRS), 63
Gems, 61–65, 66–67
General Dynamics, 172
General Electric, 82
Gold. *See* Bullion, gold; Precious metals
Grant, James, 136
Greelish, Thomas W., 135
Green, Pincus, 172
Home-Stake Production, 82–83
Hong Kong Commodities Exchange, 33
"Inside" information, 37
Institute of Certified Financial Planners, 47
International Association for Financial Planning, 47, 50
International Foundation for Art Research, 150
International fraud, 146, 152–53, 171–72
International Gold Bullion Exchange (IGBE), 8–12, 57, 61
International Organization of Securities Commissions and Similar Agencies, 171
International Postal Reply Coupons (IPRCs), 109–10
Interpol, 153
Investment
  adviser, 48, 50, 51. *See also* Financial planner(s) and planning
  Advisers Act of 1940, 48
  guidelines, 14–15
  objectives, 160–62
Investors' rights and liabilities, 23–24, 39, 90
Investor Swindles: How They Work and How to Avoid Them, 39
Invoices, phony, 23
IRS, 13, 168
Jewelry. *See* Gems
"Junk" bonds, 135–37
Justice Department, 125
Kamer, Hendricus, 77–78
Kansas Securities Commission, 87, 115
Kiting, 99
Lake Havasu City, 74–75
Lake Havasu Estates, 74–75
McCulloch Corporation, 75
Major Explorations, Inc., 85
Managed fund account, 31
Marlin, Barry, 153
Matthau, Walter, 82

191

Maturity value (of bonds), 132, 133–34, 138–39
Merchants Bank, 84
Mineral rights leasing, 88
Minnelli, Liza, 82
Mortgages, falsified, 71–72, 73–74
Moyerson, Jean–Frances, 63
Mullane, Rebecca, 151
Municipal bonds, 137
Museum of Modern Art, 149
Mutual funds, 60
National Association of Home Builders, 137–38
National Association of Personal Financial Advisors, 47
National Association of Securities Dealers (NASD), 165, 166
National Futures Association (NFA), 38, 39, 165
Nelson, Ghun & Associates, 34
Netelkos, Christos, 85–86
New-account form, 158, 162
New York Stock Exchange, 159
Nickos, Christopher J. See Netelkos, Christos
Nipp, Robert E., 73
"Nondisturbance" clause, 128
North American Bingo, 153
North American Securities Administrators Association (NASAA), 11, 12, 13, 32, 110, 133
Oil and gas drilling, 12–13, 82–91, 146–47
OPEC, 89
Options, 162
Oxborrow, Kenneth, 106–8
Pacific Chemical Products Company, 22
Palmieri, Donald, 63
"Paradise Palms Vacation Club," 123–24
Penny stocks, 85–86, 94–103, 153
Pollner, Mezan, Stolzberg, Berger & Glass, 34
Ponzi, Charles, 108–10
Ponzi schemes, 76–77, 106–14, 153
Postal Inspector, Chief, 23
Powell, Jane, 170
Precious metals, 8–12, 32, 56–61, 65–66
certificates, 59–60, 66
Precious Stones, 64
Procter & Gamble, 82
Professional Coin Grading Service (PCGS), 58–59
Prospectus, 14, 102, 154–55
for bonds, 136–37, 139
for franchises, 24–26
for penny stocks, 95–97
"Puff stocks," 169
Pyramid schemes, 71, 114–17, 171
Quinn, Tommy, 153
Racketeer Influenced and Corrupt Organizations (RICO) Act of 1970, 36
Reagan, Ronald, 137
Real estate, 70–79. See also Time-sharing
Real Estate Department, 79
Real-Estate Division, 129
Registered representative. See Stockbroker
Reliance Oil & Gas, 86
Repurchase agreements ("repos"), 135
Resources, Ltd., 83–85
Rich, Marc, 35–36, 172

Roltec, 99
St. Michael's Church of Life, 9–10
Scales, T. Carlyle, 83–84
Schuyler Stephen C., 159
Secret Service, 171
Securities, 42–43, 139, 162–63, 165. See also Bonds; Penny stocks
administrator(s), 14, 138
Commission(s), 154, 165, 166
Alabama, 83, 87, 133–34
Kansas, 87, 115
Division(s), 11
contacting for information, 66, 79, 103, 113, 129, 155
Maine, 159
New Jersey, 94
Utah, 100
Washington, 107
and Exchange Commission (SEC), U.S., 42, 44, 48, 85, 135, 171
contacting for information, 50, 103, 165
fraud, 135, 152–53, 169
Investor Protection Corporation, 166
Silver. See Precious metals
Smith, James McLelland, 94, 95, 101
Spot market prices, 11, 60, 61, 65
Stancliff, Craig, 87
Stockbroker, 158–67
Stocks. See Penny stocks; Securities
"Stripped treasury bond coupons," 133
Sundance Gold Mining & Exploration, Inc., 153
Sutton, Robert, 89–90
Swissoil, 153
Tax(es), 155
shelters, 13, 168
Telephone solicitations, 15, 37, 95–96, 101, 143. See also Boiler rooms
Time-sharing, 120–29
"Treasury bond receipts," 133
Treasury Investment Growth Receipts (TIGRs), 138
Treasury Receipts (TRs), 138
Trier Investments, 146
Trippet, Robert S., 82–83
Turner, Glenn W., 171
United States Trust Company, 82
U.S. Bureau of Land Management, 88
U.S. Congress, 89
U.S. Department of Commerce, 19
U.S. Treasury securities, 148
Utah Securities Division, 100
Fraud Task Force, 100
Veliotis, P. Takis, 172
Vesco, Robert, 172
Ward, Richard, 171
WATS lines, 144
Western Union, 82
What Else Financial Statements Can Tell Me, 166
Wheatland Investments Company, 106–8, 114
Whitmarsh, Theresa, 108
Whitney, Bernard, 77–78
Williams, Andy, 82
Winchell, David T., 153
Wiskowski, Ben, 22–23
Zero-coupon bonds, 132–35, 137–39

8218